LORD,
MAKE
US ONE

LORD, MAKE US ONE

Understanding Personalities in the Church

John W. Sloat

Judson Press ® Valley Forge

LORD, MAKE US ONE

Copyright © 1986
Judson Press, Valley Forge, PA 19482-0851

All rights reserved. No part of this publication may be reproduced, stored in a retrieval system, or transmitted in any form or by any means, electronic, mechanical, photocopying, recording, or otherwise, without the prior permission of the copyright owner, except for brief quotations included in a review of the book.

Unless otherwise indicated, Bible quotations in this volume are from the *Good News Bible,* the Bible in Today's English Version. Copyright © American Bible Society, 1976. Used by permission.

Other quotations of the Bible are from the Revised Standard Version of the Bible copyrighted 1946, 1952 © 1971, 1973 by the Division of Christian Education of the National Council of the Churches of Christ in the U.S.A., and used by permission.

Library of Congress Cataloging-in-Publication Data

Sloat, John W.
  Lord, make us one.

  Bibliography: p.
  1. Church—Unity.   2. Theology, Practical.
3. Christian life—Presbyterian authors.   4. Sloat,
John W.   I. Title.
BV601.5.S56   1986   262   86-2937
ISBN 0-8170-1101-3

The name JUDSON PRESS is registered as a trademark in the U.S. Patent Office.
Printed in the U.S.A.

In appreciation
to my family:

to Helen
   my Authoritarian

to Linda
   my Traditionalist

to Laurie
   my Transcendent

to David
   my Activist

Together they have enriched my
life and brought me completion.

Bookstore

(795

Oct 1986

73632

Contents

Preface

Have you ever disagreed with anyone in your local church on a matter of principle? Silly question. But why do disagreements happen so frequently? We all read the same Bible. Why do we come away with such different ideas about what it says? Why, in fact, can two people read the identical passage and arrive at conflicting interpretations? How can we hope for peace and unity?

We have all lived with this reality for as long as we have been in the church. Yet we have never been given a design that would help us understand the great diversity within the church. Aside from knowing that there are "liberals" and "conservatives," we may think of people as committed or uncommitted or perhaps as middle-of-the-road versus religious extremists. But why should the church have produced so many different points of view? Is there some connection among them all, some central core that binds them together in a way we have never understood?

The purpose of this book will be to present a framework into which all of the varying forms of Christian expression can be fitted. I believe that the various viewpoints found in the church fit into four basic categories.

Traditional—the desire to maintain the meaningful practices from the past, to be aware of our roots, and to protect the institutions that house and give form to the faith.

Authoritarian—the impulse to know the truth that sets us free, to find God with our minds, to accept the discipline that brings acceptance from God, and to teach others their duty to God.

Activist—the response to Jesus' demand that we care for one another, that we change the world so that it becomes more like the kingdom, and that we reduce need and suffering in the name of Christ's love.

Transcendent—the part of our nature that knows itself to be infinite spirit, that seeks to rise above the physical into fellowship with the eternal and to lift others into light and beauty.

I believe we can demonstrate that these four areas comprehend what we are called to do as disciples of Christ and that the varieties of expression we see in the church are reflections of one or more of these four positions. Various Scripture passages also refer to these four points of view, suggesting that together they form a consistent whole: traditional, Acts 2:44ff.; authoritarian, Luke 9:1; activist, Matthew 28:19; transcendent, Romans 8:9.

Many of us have a spiritual position in which we feel most comfortable. Often we think that our position is the only one or at least that it is the best. In fact, one of our major sins is being partially aware of God's plan but supposing that the part we know about is the whole truth and that those who believe differently are wrong.

We could conduct this discussion on an academic level by referring to a great variety of scholarly works on the subject, but I believe it would be preferable to think on a different level. I am hoping that pastors and church leaders, seminary students and lay people, men and women in spiritual-growth groups, the average persons in the pews, and those just beginning to ask questions about the church will use this book. Therefore, looking at the subject from the perspective of the local congregation will be more useful than an academic study.

I have served my present church for a quarter of a century. At the time I came, I was familiar with only the first two positions, the Traditional and the Authoritarian. I thought I knew a great deal about the church, but I realize now that I saw only half of the picture. During the years I have lived with these people, we have all grown. Originally, most of the members of the congregation were traditionalists, but the group has broadened to include people from all four theological positions. Sometimes our experience has been traumatic, but it has given us a much richer and more exciting vision of the kingdom. My years in this church have been a pilgrimage during which we all have slowly moved in the direction of completion and fulfillment.

Most people experience the kingdom of God through their local church. If all the members hold the same theological position, the church will be very narrow and the interaction in the congregation will be rather dull and will not stimulate much growth. The people will have little contact with those who think differently, and will tend to think of others as extremists or as people who have not properly understood the gospel.

It is essential, therefore, that each congregation learn for itself the value of the four theological positions, that it welcome into its midst those who hold views other than their own and learn from them. Only in this way will we understand the full gospel that Jesus came to preach since all four positions compliment one another and make up the whole.

I believe that what I have experienced in my own congregation has a universal application; and I invite you to take the truth in the following pages and apply it to your own church. Find among your people those who hold the traditional position, those who are activists, or those who prefer the authoritarian or the transcendent point of view. Have any of them been ignored by the majority? Has anyone been squeezed out of the church because his or her ideas didn't ''belong''? Is there an entire position missing from your church? Why is this? Because of prejudice against it or ignorance of its existence or fear about where the people who think this way might lead you?

If we are in the church to grow, we must have as many teachers as possible. Let us see what we can learn from those who sit across the aisle from us, and in so doing, let us make each local congregation a small version of the kingdom of God, where every thought is treasured and every person valued and where we all have gifts to give one another in the name of Christ.

Read and grow. And as you make your own discoveries, let me hear from you, so that together we can continue to discover even broader vistas of the kingdom.

John W. Sloat

1

Parts of the Whole

You must be perfect," demands Jesus in Matthew 5:48, "just as your Father in heaven is perfect." Have you ever tried to obey that command? For one memorable week in my life, I gave it the old college try.

At the beginning of my sophomore year in college, I decided to enter the gospel ministry. That decision was not the result of prolonged prayer but rather the culmination of a long process of weighing alternatives as diverse as dentistry and teaching, as well as the church. When the matter was finally settled, it occurred to me that I ought to pray about it and establish some warm and familiar relationship with the Almighty since we were going to be associated so closely in the years ahead. But I couldn't do it.

For one thing, I had not been much of a churchgoer in the previous year. That had been my first year away from home, and I had needed the freedom to disregard the customs of my parents for a while. For another, I was living in a fraternity house and was not exactly following the holy life. But most of all, I was uncomfortable around God. I wanted to work for God, but I didn't want to talk to God. At least, not yet.

For all these reasons, I decided to set a test for myself, which, when I passed it, would convince God of my sincerity and demonstrate my suitability for the ministry. I would live such a perfect life in the next seven days that even God would be astonished. I would do all the things I had neglected in the previous year and would avoid those things I should not have been doing. In short, I would upgrade the quality of my life with such suddenness and in such unmistakable ways that when I knocked on God's door in prayer at the end of the week, God would have no option but to let me in quickly and eagerly.

You know, of course, what happened. I got to the end of the week and realized that nothing had changed. Not one thing. What was worse,

I knew that God had been watching my struggle to improve myself. In spite of that pressure, I had not even been able to impress myself, to say nothing of impressing God.

This truth struck me as I walked past the darkened chapel on a Sunday evening. It was finally clear that my attempt to prove myself acceptable had been a subtle way of avoiding God. The truth was out and I had no more excuses. I slipped into the back pew of the empty chapel and there on my knees poured out all my confused feelings in a humbling, exalting encounter with God. We laughed together over my childish attempt to show off, and I saw that effort for what it was—a denial of the very thing to which God was calling me. When I left the chapel, it was clear that what God wanted from me was not pride about my goodness but awareness of my need. Without that awareness, I could receive nothing from God.

Perfection

This insight did not come easily. It required a complete change in my thinking. Along with most people, I had learned the subtle lesson that if I was not good, I would not be loved. I assumed that I had to earn acceptance from others by trying to do what they demanded. Perhaps this lesson is taught unconsciously by parents who, in weariness and frustration, find fear more immediately effective than love in controlling restless, inquisitive children; perhaps it comes from the basic insecurity most of us share. In any event, I experienced anxiety because I thought that acceptance by others was a tenuous thing that could be threatened by wrong behavior on my part. The command in Matthew 5, "You must be perfect," meshed exactly with what I had already learned: since the lesser authorities in my life expected good behavior from me, God, the highest authority, required the best behavior—perfection. God is perfect; therefore, God cannot tolerate imperfection. Perfection or hell, those seemed to be the alternatives. I could not go to God without wearing my best Sunday behavior because I was responsible for my own acceptability. Yet inside I was full of dread that I would not be able to maintain the pose, that God would see me for what I was, and that the game would be over.

Anyone who takes the trouble to read the gospel, however, will find overwhelming evidence that this attitude is wrong. Jesus says in Mark 10:18, "No one is good except God alone." In Romans 3:10-12 Paul quotes a passage from Psalm 14 that says, "There is no one who is righteous. . . . no one does what is right." Yet he goes on in Romans 5:8 to assert that this makes no difference: "God has shown us how much he loves us—it was while we were still sinners that Christ died for us!'' The gospel consistently tells us that our acceptance is not dependent upon our behavior but upon God's love.

But how does this relate to the verse we are discussing from Matthew 5? Read it again. Notice that when Jesus makes this statement, he does not say, "Be perfect as *my* Father in heaven is perfect." He speaks rather of "*your* Father," God, who even though perfect is intimately accessible to each of us. What a lovely touch this is! It changes the tone of the verse altogether. Thus, the verse must have a different meaning than we usually attach to it. It must refer, not to our behavior, but to our relationship with God.

We assume that the word "perfect" refers to how we act. But the dictionary defines it in terms of completeness: being whole, integrated, without defect or lack. This definition moves the concept of perfection from an active to a passive mode; perfection is not something we obtain by ourselves in isolation, but it is something that is done for us in relationship.

In John's Gospel there are several statements made by Jesus that show a hierarchy of relationships: we are dependent upon Christ who in turn is dependent upon God. Jesus says about himself, "The Son can do nothing on his own; he does only what he sees his Father doing" (John 5:19). In another place he says, "I do nothing on my own authority, but I say only what the Father has instructed me to say" (John 8:28). Jesus' perfection comes, not from good behavior, but from dependence. He needs God in order to be able to function.

In the same way, we need Christ in order to do our work. He tells us in John 15:5, "You can do nothing without me." Our righteousness comes from being dependent upon the source of righteousness, Jesus Christ, and not from acting righteously. Together, Christ and the believer form a functioning unit in the world. We need him because we are sinful and he is righteous; he works through us because he is spirit and we are flesh. When we work as one, we literally clothe his righteousness in human form. We provide the hands; he provides the truth. We are an interdependent system in which we are perfected, not by trying to prove how well we can use our hands or our brain for God, but by being part of a relationship that completes us, that gives us capabilities we were never meant to possess by ourselves.

This interdependent system of relationships operates in both directions. As we need Christ and Christ needs God, so the Divinity also chooses to work through subordinate levels of creation. God needed the incarnate Christ—in whatever sense the word "need" can be used of God—to touch the world on God's behalf, to be in the world in a way that God was not. Similarly, Christ needs us to be in the world, to continue his ministry, and to "do even greater things" (John 14:12) than he did on earth, through the power of this tri-level relationship working at its highest potential.

Perfection, then, in the sense in which Jesus used the term, does not mean trying harder; it means recognizing our incompleteness and seeking spiritual wholeness. A fuller definition of the word "perfect" is "having all the qualities that are requisite to its nature or kind." God is perfect because God needs nothing; God is complete. Our nature, however, is to be dependent upon our Creator, to be incomplete until God fills in our voids. This relationship, which allows God's nature to become our nature, adds the missing quality that completes, or "perfects," us.

Everything that follows elaborates on this basic theme: all of us— individuals, congregations, and denominations—are incomplete in ourselves, are merely parts of a larger whole. Our spiritual growth, the process of our perfecting, involves a constant search for completion— by God and by others whom God sends to teach us and to enrich our lives.

Completion

This process of spiritual growth begins when we become aware of our areas of inadequacy—the voids and blanks in our makeup—and seek fulfillment at those points. Most basically, because we are made in God's image, each of us has a God-shaped void within that can be satisfied by nothing less than God. Efforts to fill that space with money or sex or power or pleasure only leave us emptier. As Saint Augustine said, "Thou hast made us for Thyself, O God, so that our hearts are restless until they find their rest in Thee." Our need for completion, for perfecting, begins here and is built into our nature on a variety of levels.

We come to Christ partial, in process, incomplete, with gifts to offer and needs to be filled. In the church we meet others who are different from us spiritually as well as biologically and psychologically. There is a divine wisdom in that diversity: the church cannot fulfill its mission without the differences that all its members bring, because no one person comprehends the entire truth of God. But instead of valuing those differences and learning from them, we often turn away from them and write them off as deviant.

Jesus told us that two or three meeting together in his name generate a special kind of power (Matthew 18:20). When we are with others, whom we have to confront and love and listen to and learn from, we are forced to grow more rapidly. A term from atomic physics that is descriptive here is "critical mass." Certain quantities of mass, by themselves, accomplish nothing when they are separated from one another, no matter how much potential they contain. Bring them together, however, and they produce energy beyond imagining. So it is with relationships. When two or more persons are brought together, in the presence of one another something mystical happens, something is fulfilled, the mass becomes "critical," and energy is released. In the design of God, things happen in union that do not happen in isolation.

The inescapable conclusion is that God has intentionally created us incomplete. But God has surrounded us by others who, because of their differences, have the potential to complete us. Let us see who these various people are within the church.

Developing a Model

If we begin by seeing the church as a unified entity, with all its parts cooperating to create wholeness, then it will be possible to study those individual parts without wondering how each fits into the others. Let us develop a model representing the unified church in its fullness. What values are common to all Christians?

Every value in life has its opposite extreme. For example, truth and falsehood stand at opposite ends of the same line. If we were to diagram that idea, it would look like this:

Truth ___x_____ Falsehood

The x represents a particular individual at a particular point along this continuum. He is closer to truth than to falsehood, but there is still a distance for him to go. From his position on the line, we can deduce that he is a person who will tell the truth in approximately four cases out of five; but 20 percent of the time he will resort to falsehood for some reason. A person can be at only one point on such a line at a given moment, although during her lifetime she may change position many times. At any given time, there are enough people at different positions to assume that every point along the line represents someone.

We can use many such continua to plot various personal characteristics: intellectual—dull; active—passive; conservative—liberal; impulsive—cautious. To develop a diagram that will effectively describe the large variety of attitudes and behaviors in the church, we need to choose continua that will be broadly inclusive and yet highly descriptive of the essential nature of the church.

The two pairs of qualities we will use to form the model on which

our discussion will be based are LAW—GRACE and PHYSICAL—
SPIRITUAL. Why these two? For several reasons. (1) The first continuum represents the content of the message received from God, and
the second illustrates the human response to that message. (2) All four
qualities are necessary. This fact will help us answer the basic question
underlying the entire subject: Why do so many people confront the
same scriptural material and come away embracing with such emotional
fervor so many varying, even conflicting, points of view? (3) The four
qualities are all abstractions and therefore universal in their application;
they do not have a denominational or even a Protestant or Roman
Catholic bias.

The Judeo-Christian tradition and teaching provide us with a tension
between law and grace. The Old Testament taught the former, the New
Testament the latter. But it is not that simple. There is grace apparent
in the Old Testament and law in the New. We are never under one or
the other but a combination of both. Many in the Christian church are
tempted to fall back into the legalism and works-righteousness that the
gospel came to supersede; they put so much emphasis on law that grace
seems to be excluded. But at the opposite extreme it is possible to stress
pure grace to the extent that discipline vanishes. Part of growing in the
Christian faith is learning the meaning of the tension between law and
grace. We need both. But in what combination? Where we choose to
be along the continuum between law and grace says a great deal about
our spiritual perception, about our view of God.

The other dimension of the model is physical—spiritual. We begin
life conscious only of our physical nature, but our goal as Christians
is to become increasingly aware that God has also created us with a
spiritual dimension. When we discover this, we spend a lifetime answering the question, What are the implications of the fact that I am a
spiritual being in a world that is primarily conscious of physical things?
Am I to be a monk and withdraw from the physical? Am I to be a
teacher and share my spiritual insight with the world aggressively?
What does it mean that God has created me both spiritual and physical?
How am I to combine these two natures? At what point along the
continuum that connects them am I supposed to live? These are questions
with which we deal constantly as we grow, even if we sometimes
answer them by ignoring the questions altogether. No matter what we
decide, we find ourselves at some point on the line.

Since all of us are caught in the tensions created by both of these
continua, we will have two sets of forces acting on us. These forces
produce four areas into which belief systems can fall, each of the four
containing an infinite variety of subtle differences. We cannot deal with

every possible variation, but we can investigate the four major types identified by the model. Let us arrange them as follows:

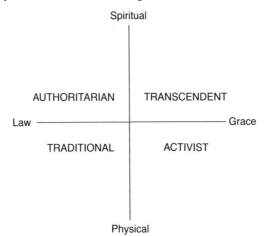

This arrangement fits our customary patterns of thinking. If the line between law and grace is thought of as a link connecting the Old and New Testaments, then using it as the horizontal continuum allows it to represent the time line between Judaism and Christianity. The vertical continuum has as its base the physical, representing our involvement in the world, and it rises to the spiritual, where fellowship with God in Christ is possible. It is common, although certainly inaccurate, to think of this dimension as vertical.

It must be made clear that a study such as this can only generalize, and that the categories discussed will of necessity be broad and inclusive. To some extent, this will help clarify the thesis by making the four positions stand out in bolder relief.

To summarize, we have considered the idea that God has intentionally created us incomplete. Rather than assume that our limited experience and understanding have revealed to us the whole range of God's truth, we need to search constantly for people whose points of view are different from our own so that they can enrich us by their distinctive insights. Our quest is for wholeness. These four areas, or various combinations of the four, fairly well represent all the varieties of theological persuasion found in the church. All are essential parts of the whole, and the model we are using demonstrates that any one position by itself is incomplete. Because we are imperfect, however, we overlook the wholeness that God has built into the church and conclude that our partial view of the truth is the entire truth.

Consider, for example, one of our habits of worship on Sunday mornings. Most of us sit in the same place week after week—right in front of the pulpit, or in the back row near the door, or halfway down the aisle by the window. Wherever it is, we feel comfortable there, sometimes unconsciously referring to it as "my pew." Because of this tendency to stay rooted in one place, we have a single point of view on what happens in the service, a unique but narrow slant that comes from sitting always in that one spot. If we are forced to move to another section of the church for some reason, we may feel oddly out of place, but we also may see things we never saw before.

In much the same way, we tend to settle down in one of the four theological positions we are discussing here because it feels more comfortable than the others. After a while it becomes a kind of intellectual "pew," the place where we have rooted ourselves, the area of the church that belongs to us. Years of viewing the church from that one angle may give us a narrow picture of what is happening, and yet we resist moving to another theological position. We may even defend our refusal to move by claiming that "my position's better than your position."

Yet no individual can have a mature, rounded faith unless there are elements of all four points of view in his or her belief system, and no local church can preach the full gospel unless it can find room under its roof for all four "pews." What this means is that the positions that are most foreign to us and that we are tempted most quickly to reject identify the areas in which we are most incomplete, in which we need most urgently to seek perfection and growth.

Let us look now at these four theological positions, searching for the one in which we now sit and looking at the others, which still have things to teach us about discipleship to Christ.

2

The Traditional Position

In 1982 my wife and I spent several weeks in Scotland, the Presbyterian "holy land." The highpoint of the visit was a pilgrimage to the Isle of Iona and its ancient abbey. Some authorities consider Iona the third most important spot in Christian history, next to Bethlehem and Jerusalem. I had heard about the place all my life but never thought I would actually be there.

Another couple flew us in a light plane from Ayrshire to the island of Mull, the largest of the Inner Hebrides, just southwest of Loch Linnhe. We landed on the east coast near Craignure on a rough grass strip frequented by flocks of sheep, which had to be buzzed and scattered before a landing could be attempted. The four of us wedged ourselves into a Morris Mini and drove west for forty miles over a one-lane road so narrow that at intervals it had passing spots in which one car was required to stop when it met another moving in the opposite direction. At the southwestern tip of the island, in the little village of Fionnphort, we caught an aging ferry that carried us across the mile of choppy sea separating Mull from Iona.

As we peered through the salt spray toward the island, we could barely make out the historic abbey, the focus of interest on the island, because its stone walls blended so perfectly with the stone terrain from which it had been formed. The ferry left us at a concrete pier at the foot of a street lined with picturesque cottages, the nucleus of the tiny permanent settlement; and we made our way uphill to the Saint Columba Hotel, a stone's throw from the abbey.

Since we were there on a weekend, we were able to worship twice in the abbey church, once at vespers on Saturday and again for Communion on Sunday morning. As we sat in the monks' stalls for vespers, we thought of Saint Columba, who had made this place famous by establishing a community of monks here in A.D. 563, and of the stupendous job of evangelism they performed by reclaiming large portions of Scotland and England for Christ, using tiny Iona as their base. In the fading light following the service, we prowled around the ruins, some of which date back almost a thousand years, and admired the beauty and antiquity of the abbey, one of the oldest remaining Christian buildings in the world. We visited Relig Oran, a graveyard said to contain the remains of forty-eight Scottish kings, including Duncan and Macbeth. We spoke with awe of the fact that a constant witness had issued from the place for three-quarters of Christian history.

In the morning we returned to the abbey church, excited at the thought of receiving the sacrament in such a historic place and assuming that the service would be dripping with propriety. We were wrong. For one thing, the Falklands War was in progress and the minister offended some of the British worshipers by criticizing the war from the pulpit. For another, the congregation of about a hundred, including a broad range of nationalities, contained quite a few children, many from the permanent community. The officiating clergyman, who appeared at first glance to look properly dour for a Scots minister, was anything but. At one point, he called the children forward and had them participate in a junior sermon, which concluded with the congregation joining them in a raucous version of "Who built the ark? Noah! Noah!" complete with clapping and laughter as the children came in "four by four, some through the window and some through the door." (They slammed the door so loudly that the whole chancel shook.)

It was astonishing. I looked around at the rude, multicolored stones and the ancient arches that formed the walls of the chancel. We were sitting here at the far end of a stream of history that Columba had begun on this spot in the sixth century. Though the current religious community on Iona was reestablished only in 1938, there had been a Christian settlement on this island for much of the past fourteen hundred years. People were worshiping here and spreading the gospel from this place a thousand years before the beginnings of our own society in the west. And yet the abbey community was still alive, filled with vitality and relevance, attracting people from around the world, still speaking forth courageously, still dealing with the people and the issues of the day. The past and the present were part of one fabric.

Then we shared Communion. In that moment I sensed at several levels what it means to be one in Christ. The worshipers had come from widely separated parts of the world, but as we sat together in that holy place, praying to the same Christ who was worshiped there fourteen hundred years ago and partaking of a sacrament instituted two thousand years ago, all barriers of nation, race, and time disappeared. We were one. The kingdom was in our midst. The saints who had once inhabited that very spot seemed to stand by us as we heard again the sacred words, "This is my body broken for you; this is my blood poured out for you." The past became real in a unique and forceful way, and I understood my debt to all those who had gone before.

The church of Jesus Christ has been in existence for two millenia. It has lasted this long because its belief has been translated into traditions that have captured its people and because its traditions have been housed in institutions and buildings and values to which they could give their hearts. Because we are physical as well as spiritual beings, we need to convert abstract concepts into concrete representations that our hands can hold even when our minds cannot always grasp the truth they represent. In the same way that God became incarnate in Christ, the teachings of Christ need to become tangible—in buildings, in books, in artifacts, in relics. Unless the mysterious takes on recognizable form, we cannot respond to it.

Thus the needs of people become symbolized in things, in structures, in traditions. This reality is represented by the lower left corner of our model, the Traditional position. This position is bounded by law and a concern for the physical. What happens when these two intersect?

The result is a set of specific concerns that are typical of a traditional point of view, housed in concrete representations: buildings, books of procedure for worship and polity, stories of past events. Among them we will consider the following: church history—what we have done in the past; church government—how we organize to create new history; church architecture—the traditional structures in which we gather to share our corporate life; liturgy—how our perception of God influences what we do; stewardship—how we underwrite the practical side of our religious life.

Church History

All living Christians find themselves at the end of a process that began with the resurrection of Jesus Christ. Without an awareness of that process, we are not truly Christian. We may be part of a local congregation and participate in the things that particular family of faith does together, but unless we see ourselves related in a direct line, through the events of two thousand years, to Jesus of Nazareth, we have missed a major aspect of what it means to profess our faith. We must, of course, find a personal, vertical, spiritual relationship with the transcendent Christ; it is this that enables us to be "in Christ." But it is the horizontal, corporate, historic stream, of which we see ourselves to be a part, that makes us "Christians."

The history of the Christian family is a long narrative in which biblical stories (many of which seem above history—almost mythological) gradually give way to accounts of the establishment of the church. This narrative begins a tiny trickle of Christian history that eventually merges with the stream of secular events and permanently colors it. This early history flows into the medieval millenium, carrying within it a powerful germ of truth that gradually spreads and affects many of the people, events, and nations it touches. As the flow continues and increasing numbers of people are engulfed by its progress, the old institutions become too constraining for the growing ferment of ideas and energy within and the structures splinter. The pace quickens and the modern era emerges, molded by those long-internalized religious principles that now become the motive for a restless surging toward progress, expansion, and freedom.

Since we are composed of both physical and spiritual natures, we need to see ourselves related to Christ on both levels, through the acts of history as well as through the ideas of faith. At the deepest level these two are inseparable. Failure to see our personal history as part of the whole range of Christian history is to separate ourselves from the family of God.

When we trace the progress of Christian history, we see the tiny light ignited in Palestine in the dusty past begin to brighten. Through the power of the Spirit and the devotion of countless disciples, it becomes a blazing light that illuminates much of the world. Between the resurrection in A.D. 30 and the middle of the second century, the New Testament was completed to serve as the authority by which the new church would confront the world in the name of Christ. When Constantine legalized the faith in 313, barely two centuries later, that fragile church had become powerful enough to conquer the empire that had come so close to destroying it. In another two centuries it had completed its western expansion to the sea and in some areas had already died out, leaving a fringe of faith on the far western coast of Europe. In the sixth century Columba and others began a movement that revisited those areas from the opposite direction, permanently replacing paganism with Christian faith. Mohammed was born in 570 and the young church was soon faced with a rival religious force; the growing strength of Islam in the following centuries was challenged by a series of Crusades, beginning in 1096. But the threats were not all external. Political struggle within the church resulted, in 1054, in a permanent rupture between its eastern and western branches. The western church continued to be wracked by turmoil, culminating in the Great Schism of 1378, when two popes attempted to rule simultaneously. John Wycliffe published his English language New Testament in 1382 and, by putting the Scriptures into the hands of lay people, set in motion cataclysmic events. A century later, in 1478, the church demonstrated how completely it had shifted from spiritual to physical goals when, in the Inquisition, it used terror to enforce loyalty to the Prince of Peace. The angry dissatisfactions that had been building for years finally erupted in 1517 when Martin Luther triggered the Reformation by calling the hierarchy to reexamine the simple truth of Christ's love. Almost exactly a century later the Puritans landed in New England searching for freedom of religion and continuing the relentless expansion of the faith. The following centuries were a time of spiritual awakening, and in our day the church, finally scandalized by the splintering of the body of Christ, has begun to move in the direction of cooperation and merger, a symbol of which was the creation in 1948 of the World Council of Churches.

This unremitting march from Bethlehem to Rome and on to a so-called Christian world is a record of ignorant cruelty as well as spiritual heroism. Yet we are Christian today because for almost twenty centuries men and women have tried to pull down the lofty teachings of Christ and incorporate them into the routine of their lives. They have made many mistakes. But history has provided us, in memory, with an enormous picture book whose pages illustrate what works spiritually to bring the kingdom closer and what denies the love of Christ and causes us to revert to new and darker forms of paganism.

Those who hold the Traditional position appreciate what has gone before and attempt to preserve all that was good and lasting from former times. This very function, however, causes them to look backward, tempting them to become defenders of the status quo. A Traditionalist was the first one who ever said, ''We've always done it that way, so why change now?''

This temptation arises because those who hold this position somehow connect righteousness with continuity. Right is defined in terms of the way things have always been done, and doing things the same way brings with it a sense of security. In a changing world at least the practices of the church can be kept from changing. So there is frequently a reactionary quality exhibited by those who inhabit this corner. Scripture can be used to beat back efforts to change traditional practices, such as ordination for men only. Lack of change may thus give a sense of permanence, but it may also have the effect of countering the revolutionary impact of the gospel. Those in this quadrant often feel that a changing world threatens everything they hold dear. Thus, they use the church to establish for themselves the stability they cannot find in the outside world. In so doing, they protect the beautiful and beloved traditions of the historic church, but they may slow down the coming of the kingdom in the present day.

Church Government

If church history is a consciousness of the things we have done in the past, church government provides the structure through which those things were done. Traditionalists can be very defensive of their particular form of government, as if they believed that *how* things are done is as important as, if not more important than, *what* is done.

Young people should be taught the structure of their own church when they prepare for membership, if not before. It is important that they have the opportunity to study diverse forms of church polity. A simple generalization is to think in terms of three major types: episcopal (governed by bishops); presbyterian (governed by elders); and congregational (governed by the local congregation). It is hoped that this comparison will help people to understand that although the systems are different, they are equally valid, scriptural, and functional.

The young people who attend membership classes in our church have been required for some time to interview a variety of clergy, asking questions that help underline the similarities and highlight the distinctions between other denominations and their own. One of the most valuable aspects of this exercise is that it provides some young people their first opportunity to speak at length with a Roman Catholic priest. Many have revealed an unacknowledged prejudice by reporting in surprise how warm, human, and cooperative these persons had been. Another value of this experience is the discovery of how much the different traditions hold in common; young people are frequently told about the differences and not the similarities.

Protestants have heard the Roman Catholic contention that the church of Rome is the only true church. Protestants, however, have been known to make the same mistake. When I first came to my present pastorate, a neighboring United Methodist congregation was served by a friendly, outgoing clergyman who was loved by the entire community. In talking with him on one occasion, I asked him to describe the strengths of Methodist polity. He startled me by responding that, in his opinion, the Methodist way of doing things was the best system in existence and that he would welcome the opportunity to prove it to me some day.

I was still a young pastor at the time; and he was twice my age and had a generation of experience in the church. In general, he seemed to be open-minded, progressive, and ecumenical, but in terms of church structure, he seemed to have an amusing blind spot.

Through the years a number of former Roman Catholics have united with our congregation, and I have had the opportunity to discuss with them the different traditions within the Protestant church. Having been brought up in what they had been told was the one true church, their early training was still whispering in their ears and they had to decide how to approach this new religious organization which, according to the former religious authorities in their life, was a nonchurch or at least a second-rate church. When they looked at the splintered state of Protestantism and compared that with the apparent unity of the world-wide Roman Catholic church, they seemed to see proof that their early instruction was correct, that the church of Rome was more authentic, more truly of God.

They were even more certain that this was true when they began to study the reasons for the differences among Protestant groups. They discovered that Methodists, Presbyterians, Episcopalians, and Baptists are different, not primarily because of what they believe but because of how they govern their churches. *How could this be?* they wondered. Why do people make so much fuss over the cover of a book? Isn't it what is inside that is more important? Then when I told them that liberals and conservatives existed in all denominations and that it was not simply a matter of one denomination espousing a liberal theology and another a conservative theology, they became even more confused. I could understand their confusion.

The fact is, however, that structure has always been needed. It was needed when Paul set apart elders in the churches he had established. Without that leadership, these churches might never have survived. Paul himself gave us the image that helps us to understand this matter most clearly. He spoke of the church as the body of Christ, with Christ serving as its head. That makes us hands and feet, arms and fingers, ears and eyes, mouths and tongues, so that working in concert we can make the entire body operate properly. But Christ is the head, the brain, the control center. Without him we are a corpse, no matter how well developed we may be.

Is not each denomination, each local church, a miniature model of this universal body? And if Christ is the head of the world church, he must also be the head of the local church. But we need to see symbols for this great mystery. That is why the Pope is called the "Vicar of Christ." He is not the head of the church; he represents Christ who is the head. Do not the pastors and officers perform the same function in the local church? Don't they help remind us of the presence of Christ?

The Greeks developed a philosophical concept which said that every physical reality is only a dim reflection of a perfect original that exists in spiritual form. The idea stated, for instance, that somewhere in the realm of spirit was the ultimate concept of "chair," and that every chair on earth was only a partial expression of that perfect original idea. Chairs were different because no one chair could completely capture the essence of the pure ideal.

There is no doubt that the same thing is true of the church. Christ set up the church, but he did not dictate details as to how it should organize itself. If its structure were an essential ingredient for the coming of the kingdom, is it not likely that he would have left us more explicit instructions? The fact that he omitted these details seems to imply that to him they were of secondary importance. He was interested, not in how the church looked, but in what it did.

Those whom he left behind, who were guided in varying degrees by his Spirit, gave form to the church simply because people needed that form. Perhaps in Christ's mind there existed the perfect form for the church, and he assumed that perfect attention to the leading of the Spirit would reveal it. It is more likely, however, that there is no perfect form but only an ideal function for the church. If this is so, then striving to develop the ideal structure is wasted effort, doomed to endless frustration since it involves searching in the wrong direction. Those looking for the perfect form are able to discover only part of the ideal, so that every formula for church organization involves some truth and some distortion. If we are honest, we must recognize that the church is partly a human invention, and as such must always be imperfect. How can we ever come to the point of saying, therefore, that any form is final or perfect or what Jesus had in mind? Our constant struggle to come closer to the truth requires that we be open to more than we have already discovered, in this area as well as in all others.

There is great tradition in churches that involve bishops and their time-honored work, great freedom in systems governed by local members and unhindered by the ties of denomination, and great democratic opportunity shared by churches that ordain lay people as elders. All have something to offer. All share differing fragments of the truth with the whole body. Each provides a sense of continuity for those who have lived for years within that system. But "if the whole body were just an eye, how could it hear?" (1 Corinthians 12:17). Fragments of the truth are not the whole truth. To canonize the form, to see the structure as more significant than the work, is to distort what Christ had in mind when he called us together into the fellowship of his body.

Church Architecture

Church buildings, and the various styles associated with those types of structures, are another element by which those who hold the traditional position maintain a sense of continuity in the world. Traditionalists often think of the church as a building rather than as a group of people committed to a mission. The building is important because it provides a base from which the people can move out to accomplish the aims of the gospel. Since God is invisible, the building becomes a representation of God's truth, giving people a concrete symbol of their identity and their connection with the eternal.

The church in which I was raised had a dark wooden sanctuary surrounded by enormous stained glass windows composed mainly of earth colors, creating a rather gloomy effect. I started to worship there with my family when I was four and remained there through high school, returning to preach as a seminarian and later as a visiting minister. The old-style stained glass, the dark woodwork, and the intricate chandeliers were an important part of my childhood view of the church; dark, quiet, holy. My parents made it very clear that a person walking into the sanctuary, even on a weekday when it was deserted, spoke softly and *never* ran. Running in the sanctuary was assumed to be, by many of us in our youth, specifically prohibited by some unnumbered commandment. All this made it clear to us that the sanctuary was a holy place and that to act indecorously there was somehow to slap God in the face. I am glad for having been taught this sense of awe about the holy mysteries of God. A sense of awe is what we mean by the word "reverence," taking God seriously, realizing that God is greater than we are, being awed by God's reality. A sanctuary is necessary; it focuses for us the presence of God. A sanctuary means a "safe place" where we can go, away from the world, in the assurance that God provides our ultimate security. But having met the God who cares for us in the high holy place, we need to carry that sense of holiness with us when we return into the world. It is our mission both to take the sacred into the mundane and to return often to that place apart where we can renew our sense of the eternal.

This association of God with place is an expression of the physical element in our model, and the rules governing behavior in that place reflect law rather than grace. These ideas are characteristic of the Traditional position. But tiptoeing around a sanctuary, which has been built by humans, and then running raucously through the woods, which have been made by God, seems to miss the real meaning of reverence. If God is everywhere, then to isolate God in the sanctuary is somehow to make it possible to avoid God elsewhere. To worship God only in the physical building is to forget that God has created the human heart as the first sanctuary.

I came to my present church about twenty-five years ago, four years out of seminary. The teaching of my youth was dying hard. The first time I saw youngsters running up and down the aisles of the church, I stopped their parents and asked if they thought this was seemly behavior. The parents, younger and more liberated than I, or at least brought up in a less traditional environment, looked at me as though they could not understand what I was asking. They talked of celebration, of the fact that the children felt at home in the church, of their joy at being part of this institution. And then one of them said, "You know, God doesn't live in this room. If they are quiet during the service, why can't they be allowed to be children during the week?" Her words made sense. I looked again at the sanctuary. It is colonial in style with white pews and Wedgwood-blue walls. Tall windows of clear glass keep the room blazing with light, in contrast to my childhood church with its perpetual darkness. Here one could sense the joy and freedom of God rather than just the mystery and distance I had associated with God in that older church. In that moment I realized that I had been subject to a tradition of man rather than a law of God. The tradition is good if it is acceptable to those who are subject to it, but it is not binding on everyone. There are other points of view that are equally valid.

Where would we be without the cathedral of Chartres, Saint Peter's basilica, or the Liverpool cathedral? We will always be grateful to those who keep these monuments to faith and piety intact so that others can look at them and be amazed at the craft of human hands, exalted by the power and creativity that devotion to God can generate in human beings. These are earthly things that come from long tradition and complicated rules about how things should be done, but they are magnificent. We would all be poorer without them.

Liturgy

If the place in which we carry out the worship of God is subject to tradition, even more so are the forms through which we worship. These forms are some of the most personal possessions of Christendom because they deal with the way we talk to God. The prayers, rituals, and liturgical forms that have been carried down through the ages unite us with our Christian forebears. Some denominations put this aspect of Christian tradition very high on the scale of values, so that the liturgy itself almost becomes sacred. It is often a major effort to revise a prayer book or modernize the forms by which people worship.

For instance, most of us learned the Lord's Prayer in the King James Version of the Bible. Yet with all the modern translations in current use, a large percentage of churches no longer use the King James Version for worship. When are we going to start teaching our children a modern version of the prayer? And when we begin, which modern version shall we use? Even if we agree that the traditional version is more beautiful than the recent renderings, it is still a fact that we no longer talk that way. Speaking to God in a different language from the one we use in everyday conversation puts God at an artificial distance from the center of life. But facing these inconsistencies will require great effort because we are so emotionally tied to the forms of the past.

At the other end of the scale from churches that use high liturgy, many Protestant denominations, especially the more conservative, have avoided elaborate ritual, sometimes because of an anti-Roman-Catholic bias. Their worship is an attempt to allow the Holy Spirit to guide them directly, and they feel that too much advanced planning tends to quench the Spirit and to limit when and how the Spirit will work. As a result the form of worship in many of these churches seems almost unplanned, spontaneous; the preacher does what the Spirit leads him or her to do at the moment, and the worshipers feel free to participate vocally at any point. Although radically different from a highly organized liturgical form, there is just as heavy an element of the traditional in this type of worship.

Many Protestant denominations have opted for what amounts to a "pop" liturgy, with an emphasis on the so-called modern way of doing things in worship: guitar music, folk songs, activist statements, interaction between people during the service, and an atmosphere of extreme informality, almost casualness. One element in this trend came a generation ago when preachers entered the pulpit and proceeded to rid the church of the language of the King James Version in public prayer. At the same time, the Roman Catholic Church was moving from Latin to the vernacular. Such changes are useful in helping worship become an integral part of daily living. We know that New Testament worship services were conducted in simply piety, using the common tongue of the day. Perhaps this is one side of worship that we should still hold as an ideal today. But there is another side. If worship is also designed to lift our hearts and help us sense the majesty of God, we must retain the beauty and grandeur of worship forms from the past—the prayers, litanies, and music that are part of our corporate heritage and are the church's gift to the present generation.

The services in the church I serve are informal and friendly but also dignified. There is a sense of family in the sanctuary; we are free to greet others, laugh, or even applaud when something touches us. Nevertheless, the invocation specifically focuses our attention on God's presence with us, and with a special intensity we stand in that awesome presence for the next hour. How we behave in that environment says a great deal about our attitude toward God.

Even so, the congregation had a memorable experience one Sunday. I have a close friend, a retired minister in the Church of Scotland, who served a congregation in Edinburgh for two decades. He comes from a heavily liturgical background and treasures the prayers and sacramental holiness that characterize worship in its finest moments. He is an Ulster Scot which means that, while he is Scottish, he speaks with an Irish accent. He was serving as visiting minister in our church on this occasion and, in addition to preaching, he read the Scripture lesson and led in prayer. The reaction of the congregation was startling and unexpected. He carried with him into the service a great sense of dignity and an awareness of the holiness of the moment that was almost tangible, and he led the service from this deep and mystical sense of the presence of God. People listened spellbound as he read the Scripture; some even wept during the prayers. They thronged him afterward to say they had never known worship to affect them so strongly. The Scripture lesson had become a high and holy moment in which God spoke to them; the prayers evoked such a sense of God's love and caring that they were lifted into a new level of spiritual awareness. They continued to speak of how they had never heard anything like this—until they noticed that I was listening. Then they smiled apologetically. But the truth had been revealed. Even people who are not familiar with traditional liturgical forms can appreciate the beauty of ancient prayers and exalted worship styles if they are delivered with conviction by someone who senses the mystery and glory of worship at its best.

What is "proper" worship? Should its content be left to the discretion of each pastor and congregation, or is there a common thread that ties all worship together? In *Varieties of Protestantism* John B. Cobb, Jr., has written:

> It is not necessary that all corporate Christian worship conform to one pattern. . . . But stemming from the command of Jesus himself, universal in the early church, and continuing unbroken to the present time, is the liturgical observance of the Eucharist as the fundamental pattern of Christian worship. Where it has been abandoned, no adequate substitute has been discovered. And, indeed, in principle we can say with confidence that no adequate substitute can ever be found, for in this liturgy alone all that is most sacred in our Christian heritage is enacted and commemorated. In it every proper response of the Christian to his God finds adequate scope, and from it all that is unworthy is excluded.[1]

This does not mean that we should celebrate the sacrament of Communion every Sunday. In fact, some of the Reformers, motivated by their anti-Roman-Catholic bias, went to the opposite extreme from daily mass and recommended that the sacrament be held once a year. The people soon discovered, however, that this was not sufficient to nourish their spiritual needs. How often and through what particular style Communion is celebrated is a matter for local decision. That it is celebrated regularly is of tremendous importance because it is in this act that the organized church in its corporate worship makes possible the closest encounter of the individual worshiper with the glorified Christ. That personal meeting, between believer and Lord, moves into the area of the transcendent position, which will be discussed later.

In our congregation we have always celebrated the Lord's Supper quarterly, in addition to Maundy Thursday and Christmas Eve. Some years ago, in response to the expressed needs of the people, we instituted a "Chapel Communion Service" at 8:30 A.M. on the first Sunday of each month. Sometimes we have twenty people in attendence; sometimes we have two. But as I serve the bread and wine to that fragment of the body of Christ, the sense of God's presence is just as real as when we share the elements in a crowded sanctuary. Sometimes it is more real.

I had an entirely different experience of Communion during a trip I took to Washington, D.C., with one of my daughters. While we were there, we went on Sunday morning to the National Cathedral, a strikingly beautiful, gothic, Episcopal church. Going forward to receive the Eucharist in that cathedral—a contrast with my normal custom of being served in the pew—provided a fresh and transcendent experience of the sacrament for me.

The immensity of the nave seemed to give my spirit space in which to swell with praise. It made me think, first, of the immense love for God of the people who built such a place and, second, of the greatness of God in contrast to my own smallness. Somehow the setting made the whole act of worship take on greater significance.

The rector invited us to share in the Holy Eucharist, explaining that since this was a national church, the table was open to every disciple of Christ. My daughter and I went forward, walking quietly down the long aisle and hearing nothing but the muffled clicking of hundreds of heels on stone, all purposefully moving toward the chancel, where waited the symbols of the sacrifice Christ made for our sake. As we knelt side by side at the altar rail, all the differences between varying traditions disappeared and what remained was the fact that all of us at that rail were brothers and sisters in Christ. The size and lavish beauty of the place somehow magnified what we were doing and touched the moment with a kind of timelessness. Together we were at the very core of what it meant to be Christian, and in a sense all of Christendom was there.

The priest came by with the wafer. I had never seen him before that day; I knew nothing about him, and as I concentrated on the wafer he held out toward me, I could not even see his face. But that moment I shared with him was intimate and deeply moving. As he stood in front of me and placed the wafer in my outstretched hands, he said, to me alone, "The body of Christ, broken for you." We both knew the significance of that moment. He was my brother in Christ; he was for me, at that moment, the presence of Christ. I had come down the aisle seeking that meeting, and he had come to me to deliver the token of Christ's sacrificial love. It was truly a "holy" moment. As another priest brought the chalice to me and helped me to take a sip of the fragrant red wine, saying to me, "The blood of Christ, shed for you," I knew what it meant for the physical to be touched by the spiritual. Jesus Christ had come to give me life. Somehow, that great cathedral served, not to make me feel inconsequential, but to increase my sense of value before God. It put everything in perspective: God's greatness, my need to come to God, and God's willingness to take my individuality seriously. I walked back up the aisle alongside my daughter, feeling exalted and full of the thanksgiving that is the heart of the Eucharist.

This was a subjective experience for me. Someone else might have had a totally different reaction to that moment, but it was a moment I shall not forget. It was not a better or a truer experience than receiving the sacrament in a small, country church; it was just different. The mystery of meeting Christ is always a profoundly personal experience. A variety of liturgical approaches to that meeting gives us the opportunity to come to it from different perspectives, to be challenged and thrilled by the freshness of it, to know that it is a living experience and not just a routine tradition. If we never make the effort to see this encounter from someone else's perspective, how very much we miss!

Persons holding the Traditional position know the importance of these moments. They need to be lifted by a type of worship that sees the invisible, hears the inaudible, touches the intangible, and lifts the heart of the worshiper into the heart of God. Because they have this need, they protect these sacred moments for those who sit in different positions.

Stewardship

To those in the Traditional corner, stewardship is a very important facet of Christian discipleship because the institutional aspect of Christian faith takes a great deal of money to maintain. In this respect, I am speaking about money given to the local church in contrast to benevolence giving for missions, something more closely related to the Activist position.

For some Traditionalists "church" means, at the very least, a group of people who meet in a building. Take away the building and some people in this corner become confused about how to define themselves. A few may even wonder whether they are a "church" any longer.

A decade before I came to my present church, the members of the congregation had lost their church building as a result of a devastating fire. It was a traumatic experience for the people, particularly because the fire happened on Saturday night. A number of people came to worship at eleven o'clock the following morning only to discover the truth when they stood before the blackened and smoking remains. They worshiped in a YMCA building down the street that morning, amid tears and serious questions about their future as a church.

For three years, while the new building was being erected, the congregation met for worship in a Masonic Scottish Rite Cathedral, during which time the membership dwindled from one thousand to less than six hundred. The group did not have its own church building, and it was difficult for many in the community, especially newcomers, to think of the congregation as a "real" church. Four hundred souls fled into the night, many, I believe, finding it hard to conceive of a church without a building.

I would be the last to undervalue the importance of a house of worship, but when we deal with stewardship, we face the fact that a large part of our church contributions go to maintain the physical plant. In many cases it almost seems that the mission of the local church is to keep its building in working order. That is not how I read the New Testament. We have put our own interests ahead of the interests of those to whom Christ has sent us. We have a need to be too modern, too comfortable; we long for new and more lavish conveniences. We spend so much time and love and money on our church edifices that it is no wonder that they become an end in themselves, at the expense of the church's outreach. I have pointed out to the leadership in my church that if only we were free from this building and its constant demands upon us for time and money, we could establish such a creative ministry that it would dazzle the community. But they look at me as though I am blaspheming. They struggled and sacrificed for years to erect this building, they remind me. And anyway, what is a congregation without a church?

Looking over our current budget, I see that about one third of our income is used simply to maintain the building. Though this proportion varies considerably, our commitment to our buildings is very high and we need to evaluate this cost against what we gain from the expenditure.

Are we in the discipleship business to own real estate or to evangelize and educate? The New Testament church conducted a powerful evangelistic movement without owning "church property." Is there something we can still learn from them?

Those who hold the Traditional position are interested in the visible aspect of the church and feel that obeying God involves maintaining the old institutions and preserving the practices that have meant so much in the past. They perform a valuable function for the whole church. These things, if left to the more otherworldly among us, might soon disappear.

3

The Authoritarian Position

When I finally decided to enter the ministry, one of the first things I wanted to do was to tell one of my uncles about my decision. He was an ordained minister in another denomination.

I lived only thirty-five miles north of Princeton, N. J. My pastor, who had always prayed that I would enter the ministry, had graduated from Princeton Theological Seminary. My father was a graduate of the famous university in that town. As a result, there was little question as to where I would go to seminary. Since it is the oldest school in our denomination, I expected no objection on the part of anyone to my decision to attend there.

But when I told my uncle of my decision to enter the ministry, the first question he asked was, "Where are you going to seminary?" As soon as I told him I was considering Princeton, he began a lecture on the failings of that particular school and on the fact that studying there could not prepare me adequately for a life of service in the church. He proceeded to tell me that I should take this matter seriously enough to get a decent theological education for myself, one that could be obtained, of course, at the seminary he had attended.

I went to Princeton, but while I was there this kind of communication continued. On one occasion he sent me a magazine, the official organ of his denomination, that contained an article written by him. In the article, which involved an attack on Princeton Seminary, he concluded by saying something to the effect that the future of the church did not lie with the seminary or its misguided president. In later years he has spoken of his total aversion to my denomination. Others have quoted him as having said, in his earlier days when he was in a position of authority, that one of the duties of pastors in his denomination should be to locate churches next to existing mainline congregations in order to counteract their theology and be a witness for truth in that area.

Now, admittedly, this example is extreme, but I do not think that it is atypical of the thinking of many in the church. People who hold viewpoints similar to that just described are Authoritarians. So are many others whose views are a good deal more tolerant.

Authority is essential. Christian discipleship is primarily obedience to God, who is the ultimate authority; to reject God's authority is to sin. Without some degree of authority the church could not continue. But if authority is wielded without concern for the needs of individuals, it becomes tyrannical, a detriment to the kingdom. The same thing can be said about each of the four positions being described: each has a valuable contribution to make but, allowed to grow out of proportion, it becomes destructive.

The second corner of our model is bounded by law and the spiritual. It is inhabited by those who desire a close relationship with God in Christ but who see that relationship constrained by the demand to define clearly what God requires of us. We can divide the Authoritarian position into four areas: scriptural interpretation, theology, Christian education, and church discipline.

As I have said, all four positions are necessary to the fullness of the church of Christ, and I mean to point out their value for all of us. Yet any positive value can be distorted, and I will also attempt to illustrate the ways in which these qualities have been misused.

Scriptural Interpretation

The heart of Christian faith, and certainly the core of denominational integrity, rests upon scriptural interpretation. Protestants see Scripture as the only rule of faith and practice, and some go so far as to say that it is the infallible guide by which we must be led. Scripture contains within it the authority of God, since Christianity is a revealed religion. God is revealed through the Word; by disregarding what it says, we disregard God.

As a result, interpretation of the Bible has always been of prime importance. Practically any verse of Scripture is open to interpretation, and we look for someone to help us understand its "true" meaning. This creates an important role for those skilled in interpretation. The alternative is for everyone to follow his or her own interpretation, which leads to chaos. Or does it?

Differences in interpretation have usually been responsible for the establishment of new denominations. We tend to cluster with those who believe as we do. If we differ over what Jesus meant by baptism, for instance, we can separate into groups based upon those differences. One group reasons from reading the Bible that since Jesus was immersed, he meant for everyone to be immersed. But another group argues that the spirit of the sacrament and not the form is what is important; therefore, it is permissible to sprinkle as long as it is done in the name of the triune God.

Then we discover that we have two different practices, each based on Scripture according to its proponents. Some immediately react by saying that this cannot be. God cannot contradict God; therefore one of the practices must be wrong. Those who hold that there can be only one right interpretation of Scripture will declare, of course, that their particular interpretation is the most accurate. This leads to the conclusion that they have a way of interpreting the Word of God that is superior to others. They defend this conclusion by asserting that the Holy Spirit gives them the interpretation and that any attack upon their view is therefore an attack upon God.

My uncle was so convinced that my denomination was not based on Scripture—that its members read one thing in the Bible and do something else in practice—that he refused to come to my ordination. He stated that he did not wish to see me take vows that I had no intention of keeping. I fully intended to keep every vow I took at my ordination; but my view of keeping them differed from his, and so he assumed I was wrong and he was right.

People have been studying the Bible for many centuries. They have been coming to different conclusions for that entire time. Part of the reason for this is that the truth of God is far too vast to be reduced entirely to writing. Our human minds can never fully grasp the wholeness of God and God's plan for us. Further, Jesus clearly told us that the Bible does not include the whole truth about God's plan for us. He said, "I have much more to tell you, but now it would be too much for you to bear. When, however, the Spirit comes, who reveals the truth about God, he will lead you into all the truth" (John 16:12-13). This means at least two things: first, each person perceives God in a slightly different way, and therefore his or her response to God is personal and distinctive; second, since the Bible is to be supplemented by the witness of the Holy Spirit, each of us hears some slightly different aspect of the truth.

I believe that God not only is pleased by this but has planned it this way. We are all colorful fragments in a giant mosaic of truth, and each of us has something unique to contribute. Our insights are, therefore, not mutually exclusive or threatening; they are gifts we have to offer one another through the Holy Spirit. To ignore another person's gift is to turn our back on some piece of the truth God holds out to us. As a result, two ideas that appear to be contradictory may both be right because they are both partial and fragmented pieces of a much larger picture.

This may sound as though we are recommending chaos, but this does not have to be. Each of us is responsible for what we believe God is saying, not for what someone else tells us God is saying. To state that there is only one interpretation of truth is to say, for instance, that Roman Catholics are right and Protestants are wrong. We cannot say that. Some would say, then, that the only alternative is to believe that there is more than one truth. That cannot be, unless God is not God. Thus we must come to the conclusion that none of our interpretations are complete and that the problem lies in our temptation to claim that our partial understanding is the entire truth. This is the theme that is repeated in small details and large rhythms throughout this book. If we claim that our partial human understanding is equal to the whole truth of God, then we put ourselves in the place of God; we become the authority instead of remaining under God's authority. That is blasphemy. If our interpretations, then, are not complete in themselves, we must be dependent upon the insights of others to fill the gaps in our own knowledge. By distancing ourselves from those who believe differently than we do, we insulate ourselves from the very information that will help to make us more complete.

For example, some people picture God as punishing and harsh, while others speak of God as loving and infinitely forgiving. They are both wrong simply because they are both only partially right. Both points of view can be substantiated from Scripture, but to maintain that God is all one or the other is to ignore the evidence. Perhaps some are better at understanding the wrath whereas others can document the grace of God in more detail. By concentrating on its facet, each group helps develop useful information for us all. But by itself neither group paints the whole picture. Each needs to inform the other, and neither can be complete without the other. The same is true with all scriptural interpretation. The conservatives and the liberals, the Protestants and the Roman Catholics, all have something to share with one another. None of us are wise enough to understand it all; to claim that we are is to demonstrate a form of sin.

As humans we are not built with the ability to see both sides of a mountain at the same time. Therefore, while we are viewing one side, we must accept the witness of others concerning what is happening on the other side at that moment. Why not also accept this fact in relation to the holy mountain of scriptural truth? To see only our side is to rob ourselves of the experience of others and to miss some of the beauty of God's truth.

Theology

Once a group has decided how it is going to interpret Scripture—whether it will follow the literal meaning or the spirit of the teaching—it sets out to formulate a consistent theological position by using that interpretation of Scripture to shed light on various areas of human life and activity. A church that holds a harsh and authoritarian view of God, for example, is likely to have a low view of human beings, which states that they are lost sinners in need of redemption or punishment. On the other hand, a theology that describes God as merciful and forgiving is unlikely to have a detailed description of a hell in which God punishes sinners eternally.

Paul took the teaching of Jesus and the traditions of the early believers and formulated them into a unified theology. He spoke of many things not specifically touched upon by Jesus because the church was beginning to need a comprehensive statement of what the Christian life involved. For instance, what did a person's Christian faith have to say about his or her marriage? Should it be different from those of people outside the church? Paul, as a good lawyer, tried to answer this and many other fine points of interpretation so that members of the Christian community could have help in trying to live lives patterned after Christ.

Unfortunately, in the matter of marriage, Paul changed his emphasis as his understanding of the world was modified. At first he believed that the return of Christ would happen almost immediately, and so he recommended against marriage. He believed that it was better to keep oneself untangled from these demanding relationships so as to be able to concentrate on serving Christ and preparing for his coming. He said such things as, "A man does well not to marry" (1 Corinthians 7:1); "To the unmarried . . . I say that it would be better for you to continue to live alone as I do" (1 Corinthians 7:8). He made a concession, however, to those who could not restrain themselves, saying that in extreme circumstances, if one was burning with passion, it was better to marry than to be consumed by the passion (See 1 Corinthians 7:9). This was a point of view that did not see marriage as a priority or regard it in sacramental terms. Nevertheless, when Paul finally concluded that he would not see the return of Christ during his physical lifetime, he restated his attitude toward marriage, saying that it was a holy estate based on the relationship between Christ and the church (see Ephesians 5:25-32). He saw clearly that if the church were to continue it would have to reproduce itself, and celibacy worked against this end.

Now, it might seem that he was saying two opposing things: marriage is to be avoided if possible, and marriage is one of the highest of all spiritual relationships. Which one did he really believe? Or did he

decide that both were true under different circumstances? Various conclusions have been reached across the years. Some groups took Paul
literally and did not marry, thereby condemning themselves to eventual
extinction. Those who see the Bible as literally inspired cannot imagine
Paul changing his mind, since that would mean that God had not been
clear when he first inspired Paul. As a result, they might say that when
it appears that Christ's return is imminent, people should refrain from
marriage, but that in the meantime it has God's blessing. More liberal
theologians, however, would simply say that theology is an incomplete
body of information about God and that as we grow spiritually, our
ideas mature. Their view would be that as Paul learned the plan of God
more fully, his thinking changed and he gained a long-term rather than
a short-term perspective on Christian discipleship.

When the evidence of Scripture is run through the mills of various
theological minds, it comes out bearing the mental teeth marks of the
individual thinker. It must be this way. Since we are all different, it is
inevitable that we will all see God in varying ways. What this means
is that God is the God of the individual: each one of us must come to
God individually, relate to God's love one at a time, and answer to
God by ourselves and for ourselves. Our theology, therefore, must
ultimately be a personal theology, not simply a parroting of the church's
theologians.

John Calvin, Martin Luther, the Wesleys, and other great thinkers
of the church did us a lasting service by shining the light of Scripture
through the brilliant prisms of their minds. They refracted the truth of
God into its various components and brought a unifying eye to divine
revelation, which most of the rest of us could never do. But while their
thinking can be of help in developing our own ideas of what God is
like and what God requires of us, we may never be able to accept every
detail of the conclusions at which they arrived.

The Pharisees of the Old Testament were lawyers, specialists in the
law of God. They wanted so sincerely to please God that they tried to
anticipate every possibility for disobedience, hoping that they could
avoid even involuntary breaking of the law. They wanted to know every
tiny implication: What does the law imply about my relations with
women? What can I deduce from it about wearing false teeth on the
sabbath? How can I most perfectly obey God? Their work and their
zeal grew out of a positive desire to be perfectly obedient to God.

The apostle Paul was a lawyer, a Pharisee, a person trained in applying
the laws of God to every detail of daily living. It was inevitable that
he would ask searching questions about how the new faith affected
people's lives. In the process, he could not prevent his own background

from creeping into his work and influencing his ideas. His attitude about women is one illustration. My own opinion is that God does not desire women to keep silent in church (see 1 Corinthians 14:33-34), that God sees all of us, regardless of our sex, as equally valuable and capable of leadership. So there are points at which I must depart from Paul's thinking when I feel that my deeper sense of the will of God makes some of Paul's conclusions archaic. That does not mean that I throw out everything that Paul said, although some will claim that to discount any of it undermines the authority of all of it. What it does mean is that I have to search it all, carefully, for myself, and decide where I can be instructed by it and where I have to disagree with it. That is a much heavier responsibility than merely accepting all of it, unthinkingly and uncritically.

John Calvin was a lawyer, and his lawyer's mind wanted to reduce religious knowledge to a law so basic that it would make everything else fall into place in a perfectly cohesive system. He found that fundamental law in the idea of the sovereignty of God. If God is totally in charge of creation, then God can do anything; our relationship to God is severely limited by God's power and our weakness, by God's parenthood and our dependence. Using this foundational idea, Calvin developed not only a concept of God but doctrines about man in relation to God, about sin, about the nature of salvation, about the work of the church, and so on. If such a comprehensive study of the impact of Christian faith upon human life is not attempted, how are we to know who we are as Christians and what we are to do? If a non-Christian asks you what it means to be a follower of Christ, how do you answer that person unless you have some sort of a creed to summarize your beliefs? Without one, the only thing you could do would be to quote Scripture, no part of which by itself is sufficiently comprehensive.

Everyone should read Calvin's *Institutes of the Christian Religion* and other great doctrinal formulations and learn from them in order to enlarge and clarify his or her own thinking. But again, neither Calvin nor anyone else can think for us. Others can only aid us in our own thinking. While I agree with Calvin's stress on the sovereignty of God, I cannot accept all the implications that he sees flowing from the concept. His belief was that God's sovereign power leaves God free to condemn some people to hell for His own glory, regardless of how they live their lives. This may be a perfectly logical conclusion and may create a beautiful consistency in his system of ideas, but I think it crowds God into a bed that is cut much too small. There is a great deal in Calvin that will always be of value; but if we are maturing spiritually, it is inevitable that we will outgrow some of his ideas. We should not be afraid of this, because our object is to grow toward God, not to settle down forever with a single point of view.

When I was writing a master's thesis some years ago, I interviewed a number of clergymen to discover how individual faith comes into being. One of the men with whom I talked at length was a thoroughgoing Calvinist who jokingly claimed that he saw Calvin as third only to Jesus Christ and the apostle Paul. He wanted to be carefully organized in his religious thinking so that he could assure himself that he had brought the best of his critical judgment up against the most important truths of God. He wanted to know what he believed, and he wanted to be able to tell others in compelling and thoughtful terms what he believed. But he also had a sense of perspective. He said in a very revealing moment,

> Sometimes we Calvinists tend to make a god of our creeds. If we can get our creed tight enough, polished enough, perfect enough, so that it really comprehends the truth of God, then we're happy. Sometimes we get to the point where we don't even need the Holy Spirit. We feel that we have the whole truth in our heads and down on our papers.

You can imagine, then, how amused I was to hear a Pentecostal minister say in a later interview, "When we are swept away in the inspiration of the Holy Spirit, he gives us everything we need for Christian life and salvation. Sometimes, in the ecstasy of the Spirit, we get to the point where we feel we don't even need the Bible." They were both saying that we are all tempted to make gods out of our particular point of view. But God wants to enlarge our view of things, and that enlargement often comes through those who have a different theological stance from our own.

Jesus said, "If you obey my teaching, you are really my disciples; you will know the truth, and the truth will set you free" (John 8:31-32). I believe that God's truth *is* designed to set us free. But what is the truth? Ever since Jesus made that statement, we have been trying to define the truth about which he was speaking. We believe that being a good disciple means working hard at knowing the truth, not just living an unexamined life in the faint hope that it will somehow be acceptable to God. And once we think we have found the truth, we try to get others to accept it. If, after all, what we teach is the truth, then must not others accept it for their own good? When we urge others to accept the truth as we see it, are we thinking of them or of ourselves? The fact is that when someone disagrees with us, it casts doubt upon our point of view. We can either remain in doubt, give up our viewpoint, or convert the other person, since agreement will strengthen our own position. It is very hard to separate ego from truth.

Some institutions function on this level, and some individuals find it safer to let the institution do their thinking for them. The Roman Catholic church is one example, but so are some conservative Protestant denominations. They say in effect, "Let us tell you God's truth; then do as we tell you and we will guarantee your salvation. After all, we are the professionals in religion, so you must listen to us." The facts that these institutions have endured for many years and that some are even growing in strength at present indicate that there are many who desire this kind of theological supervision.

We need to be guided by authority, and the church is a visible reminder that God is the ultimate authority for us all. But the truth sets us free, according to Jesus. As we seek that truth, we must be certain that we do not slip into bondage to a new Pharisaism.

Christian Education

Christian education is the third facet of the authoritarian corner, the means by which denominational theology, once it is formulated, is transmitted from one generation to the next.

Teaching is the heart of the church's mission. Jesus was a teacher. He came from God to reveal that God loves us and wants us to love in return. Teaching is walking in the steps of the Master and passing on the knowledge that God loves everyone. In my denomination the ministers were formerly called "teaching elders." I always treasured that title. It clarified my function and reminded me daily that I am a follower of the greatest teacher.

Teaching is the direct descendant of the first two facets of authority. First comes scriptural interpretation, then the formation of a theology based on that interpretation, and finally the effort to educate others in that Christian theology. As a result, the type of educational style used will be a direct outgrowth of the group's attitude toward authority.

Education can be viewed in two ways by the church. It can be seen either as indoctrination (filling supposedly empty minds with the teacher's ideas, since he or she is the authority) or as a means of helping people to think for themselves. These two approaches are direct opposites, the former tending to be used more heavily by authoritarian groups.

I believe that teaching people to think for themselves is the superior method. Since salvation is the result of working out my own personal relationship with God, I have to struggle with the ideas of faith for myself. If I accept someone else's thinking without ever asking if those ideas make sense to me, I will always be wearing a garment of faith not tailored for me. This does not lead to spiritual growth.

As teachers, we need to be growing constantly in faith and knowledge. We cannot teach what we do not know, although the church, by using untrained teachers, is more guilty of attempting to do this than most institutions. I will never forget an experience I had early in my ministry. I happened to be in the church library on a Sunday morning during the church school hour. On the other side of the free-standing library shelves, a class was meeting in which a woman was trying to instruct third and fourth graders about the patriarch Joseph. She recounted the story in bare outline and told how, even though his brothers had been cruel to him, God was going to use him in an important way. She asked expectantly, "And you know what God had in store for him, don't you, children?" *Sure,* I thought to myself, picturing him in regal Egyptian garb, *God made him second in authority to the pharaoh.* "Surely, you know what happened to Joseph," she persisted. "Joseph? Well, he became the father of Jesus!"

I almost let out a shout and I had to restrain myself from calling out a correction over the top of the library shelves. But that would have revealed that I had been eavesdropping and I didn't want to embarrass the teacher. I have never forgotten that shocking moment. It made me aware of how questionable some of our education may be, perhaps no more than shared ignorance. What does that say about how effectively we are training the next generation in the church?

But the same thing is also true for me. As much as I treasure my title of teaching elder, I am aware of my shortcomings. What responsible teacher is not? Even if the scriptural interpretation and theology of my denomination were flawless, I would still be a flawed communicator of its perfection. I teach my own fears, my own prejudices, my own unfounded hopes. I teach as I see the truth, but that may not be as God sees it. Even if my perspective is reasonable and accurate, it may not be a view that is helpful to the student at that moment. Teaching at its best must be witness, sharing what I have experienced for what it is worth, without the assumption that my view is going to be the most useful view for everyone else. And that is evangelism; we will deal with that when we discuss the activist position.

Most other elements of teaching come under the authoritarian heading. But how do I, as a teacher, use that authority? For instance, when I am teaching a class on Exodus and I come to the eighth commandment, which says, "Thou shalt not steal," what do I say next? I have two choices. I can cite all the instances in which the commandment applies, tell the students how they should comply, summarize the church's position on the issue, and instruct them that they are duty-bound to accept all that I have told them. Or I can simply set the facts before them and ask them how they view the matter. I can give my opinion, tell them why I think that way, even debate with them when we disagree. But if I believe that they are ultimately responsible to God for their own faith, then I must conclude that it is my duty as a teacher to help them hammer out their own faith and not to think for them. If I believe in the priesthood of all believers, then no matter how exalted a teacher I may be, I must remember that they may also have something to teach me through the work of the Holy Spirit.

When we teach in the church, we need to ask ourselves: Have I learned it all, or am I still discovering new truth from God? The answer will have a great impact on our teaching.

Church Discipline

Finally, under the authoritarian heading, we must deal with the matter of church discipline. Discipline is clearly an aspect of authority, but the Authoritarian position in our model—a function of law and the spiritual—reminds us that discipline is an attempt to enforce on earth the spiritual values of heaven. Is it realistic to think that this can be done?

The elders in my first church delighted to tell me of a case in earlier times when a member of the congregation had been hauled before the assembled elders and tried on charges of stealing corn from a neighbor's field. He was put out of the church until he showed repentance for his act.

The elders, in repeating the story, were reminded both of their potential power and of how much things had changed since then. As one said, "We wouldn't even think it was the business of the elders to consider such a matter today." But why? Right and wrong certainly have not changed. If it was right to discipline a member for such an act back then, why is it unnecessary today? This implies that we may be wrong today in some of the things we enforce, and that at some later date we may look back upon our current decisions and think ourselves to have been foolish. If we refuse to deal with these situations today because of our greater permissiveness, perhaps we need to understand that we are guilty of rejecting the discipline of God.

Although I laughed with the elders over the incident, I was faced with such a situation during that pastorate. It came to my attention that one of the church's elders was having an affair with a woman in the church. Rather than act on rumor, I asked him to come to my study to discuss the matter. I was surprised when he brought the woman in question with him. They freely confessed everything, stating that they were in love and were hoping to be married. I reminded them that at the moment they were each married to someone else and that the seventh commandment said nothing about future intentions nullifying its prohibition. I told him directly that unless he broke off this illicit relationship immediately, I would take steps to have him removed from his church office, a move that would have caused him some personal embarrassment. He agreed, not because he thought I was right in making the demand, but because he feared that the notoriety would hurt his business. I had wielded the church's power, and I had prevailed. I discovered later that he had merely become more discreet, had continued the liaison, and eventually married the woman.

I was twenty-five years of age at the time; he was twenty years older than I. How much was I constrained by the demands of ego to exert my power, and how much did I hope to make him see the error of his ways? Are threats liable to make a person more spiritual, more deeply accountable to God? I wonder how power is to be wielded so that it accomplishes its purpose without simply hardening the resistance of those on whom it is used. Is it designed to make a sinner repent, to provide someone as a bad example for the rest of the faithful, or just to make those in authority feel superior?

The shoe was on the other foot some years later when I was the subject of censure by some of the elders in my present church. It was during the 1960s and there was a great deal of dust being stirred up in the churches by conflicting attitudes toward the endless war in Vietnam. A college just north of our town was offering draft counseling for young men in the vulnerable age category. The purpose of the counseling was not to urge them to break the law but to help them understand it more fully so that, knowing their options, they could make informed decisions. Some of the ministers in the area were polled for the names of men who might benefit from the counseling and, in the process, were asked if they approved of the program. I indicated that I did.

Not long afterward two of my elders came to the study and said solemnly that they wanted to talk about something serious. They had heard that I was counseling young men to break the law. Both of these men, friends of mine then and now, are authoritarian types—conservative, clear in their minds about what they consider to be right and wrong, and not interested in seeing the boat rocked. I was stunned by their presence and by the obvious gravity with which they viewed the situation. Instead of answering immediately, I asked them to tell me what they meant by "breaking the law." They explained that informing young men that they had any option other than obeying a draft notice when it arrived constituted, helping the young men to break the law and made the minister involved a lawbreaker as well. Again I asked them a question: "What would your response be if I said I was involved in doing what you describe?" They answered that they would have to ask for my immediate resignation.

Their answer fell on me like a rock. I knew that there were ministers who were being persecuted because they backed unpopular causes, but I had never thought of this happening to me. Besides, what I was doing seemed so bland, so obvious an example of free speech, that I hadn't even looked on it as controversial. But they saw it as a threat; they felt it their duty to tell me that, as far as they could see, I was being unchristian and unpatriotic.

Here was the other side of the use of power. In the past I had used my authority and position to threaten a philandering elder. Now the elders were using theirs to threaten me. I knew it was hard for them to do, but it was revealing to see that they felt so strongly about the matter that they were willing to risk the friendship. As Authoritarians they felt that being right was more important than being friends. I respected them for that, but I was angry with them at the same time. What they did took courage, but I thought that their point of view was elementary. I believe I responded, heatedly, that I was doing exactly what they were accusing me of and that the next move was theirs! Then, after I calmed down, I explained my reasons for being part of the counseling. Whether I changed their minds or not, I may never know. I heard nothing on the subject from them again, but it was a significant lesson for me. I realized that I am not the only one who can speak with authority, who can wield power. How do I react when someone tries to coerce me, especially when I think his or her ideas are wrong? How, then, do I suppose someone else reacts when I try to use my authority to change his or her mind? Can power ever be used to teach the truth, or is that a useless exercise?

There is much talk in the church now concerning the ordination of women. Our denomination has decided that not only is it right but it is required. Churches seeking pastors must affirm that they would interview women candidates, and all churches must have women elders. Some ministers and some churches believe, in good conscience, that this is not proper. They want the right to disagree with the majority. They are convinced that the denomination is wrong in ordaining women, but they think a far greater wrong is being committed when the denomination forces them to do something that is contrary to their consciences. The denomination holds the power. It can refuse to allow a pastor to serve a church if he does not state that he is in favor of ordaining women, and it can use other means to enforce its will if a local church refuses to add women to its ruling board.

The question behind discipline is this: Can we *force* people to be Christian? On the other hand, can we have a denominational system if there is not some way of forcing compliance to the will of the majority?

Authority says, ''You must do this; you must not do that.'' Authority is the voice of the majority. But does the majority always rule in spiritual matters? Did it rule in Jesus' day or at the beginning of the Reformation? If we must all find our own way to God, if each one must answer for herself or himself to God, what happens to the minority if it follows a course with which it does not agree simply to keep peace within the denomination?

Discipline is necessary within the church, but it must be the discipline of God, not of human beings. There lies the real test of Christian grace: How do we wield the authority of God and yet remain humble?

4

The Activist Position

I had been in my present church only a few years when the great 1963 civil rights rally was held in Washington, D.C., the rally that ended with Martin Luther King, Jr., giving his memorable speech, "I have a dream. . . ." Before the rally one of the older pastors in town told us that he had a strong desire to be there. We listened with mixed emotions because at the time, especially in conservative areas, this whole event was suspect.

Our colleague was not particularly flamboyant or progressive, not noted for his political activism or even his liberal views. Yet somehow he knew he had to be there. Some of his friends urged that he stay home. After all, he was pastor of the main downtown church, a staid and traditional congregation that could only view such behavior on his part as radical. Some of us may have felt that it would make us look bad if this older pastor went while those of us who were younger, and supposedly more sympathetic to the civil rights battle, stayed home. He asked me personally if I wanted to go with him, but I found some excuse. I really had to stay home with my family and my people; the Lord needed me here—you know the line.

He ended up going by himself, and he came back a different man. He had faced his own fear and won. He had not backed down in the face of hostility from his congregation. Later, he preached a forceful sermon on the experience, even though this meant reminding the congregation of what he had done. He needed to stand up and be a witness to what had happened.

He said to me after he returned home, "I feel as though I have been to the mountain top, too, and seen the other side. You can't put into words what it meant to be there. It was a whole new view of the church, of the kingdom of God, of what it means to be Christian. The people who were there were committed people; they were taking risks to put their faith into action. You knew that they meant what they said. And somehow you gained strength from the crowd. There was power there that I have never felt before. It energized me. I now see things I never saw before. If I hadn't gone, I would be less of a person and less of a Christian.''

There was a mystical quality to his recounting of this event, a sense that he had seen a land that few others have experienced. He knew that he could never quite describe it to us because we hadn't been there. I began to regret my quick refusal. He had taken a chance and had won. I had played it safe and had been left out.

I have never forgotten that moment. It made me understand that there is a lot more to Christianity than institutional routine.

The Activist position is bounded by grace on the one hand and by a concern for the physical on the other. Together these two concerns ask the question, How do we make the grace of God felt in the world? Those who hold the Activist position are in good company. Jesus was an activist. Paul was an activist. Martin Luther and Martin Luther King, Jr., were activists. They were all convinced that God wanted the *status quo* changed. If it were not for their work, we would not be who we are today.

Activism can be divided into four areas for our study: program, evangelism, special ministries, and justice.

Program

It may be hard to think of a normal church program as an activist approach to Christianity, but we must remember that until recently practically all of the church's institutional program was held on Sunday morning and consisted of Sunday school and morning worship.

A few years ago when I was writing a history of our local congregation, I telephoned one of the church's former pastors. He was living in a nursing home in Cincinnati, was eighty-five years of age, and was confined to a wheelchair. I wanted to talk about his work during the years he served the church, from 1920 to 1925.

He spoke of the things he had done as a pastor, telling me that he had made more than a thousand home visits in the congregation in a single year. To be polite I responded, ''Well, I certainly don't make that many calls.'' That was all he needed. ''I know you don't,'' he shot back. ''I don't know what you young fellows do with all your time. In my day we knew what we were there for. I was called to preach and to make visitations. And that's what I did.''

Somewhat chastened, I asked, ''Weren't there programs in the church that you were required to attend?'' Immediately he answered, ''The pastor carried the program to the people. You worked with them in their homes. You encouraged the backsliders to come to worship; you counseled them about marriage and death; you read the Scriptures to them and prayed with them. I worked hard at that, and I didn't even have a car. If I couldn't get a ride, I took a trolley; if that didn't go where I wanted to go, I walked. You fellows couldn't survive in that kind of a ministry. You're too busy running a three-ring circus in the church today.''

Well, I had asked for it. Apparently he had wanted to get that off his chest for a long time. He was upset because things were no longer as they had been. Our styles of ministry were very different.

Is that what we run in our churches these days, a three-ring circus? By trying to provide a little something for everyone, are we really neglecting our basic ministry? Is the church intended to be a three-course, sit-down banquet or a stand-up buffet? or should it be a little of both?

Some people in our congregation complain that being a member of the church is a full-time job. They are here four or five times a week for hours at a stretch. During one week some time ago, our young people were preparing a play for worship at the same time they were participating in a hunger fast. A few parents called to complain that their children were spending too much time in church. Imagine that, in this day and age! The young people weren't complaining, but the older folks could not imagine a program so exciting that it made their children want to be there every day.

Should the development of such a program be our goal? I can re-member dreaming with other seminary students about the earth-changing programs we were going to develop when we finally had churches in which to work. It seemed to me at the time that the feverishness of one's program had a direct connection with how soon the kingdom of God would come. Program was everything. One of my professors said admiringly that we front-line pastors were the only generalists left in the profession. In a day of specialization we parish ministers have to be able to do a little of everything. We came out of seminary believing that by sheer energy we could make our churches successful and achieve heaven on earth.

As a result I have spent years editing newsletters, creating midweek meditations for distribution, teaching classes, meeting with committees, counseling, developing special interest groups, writing communicants' class material, and so on; all this was in addition to what I was ''supposed'' to be doing—preaching and calling. And this was only in my church life. In the community I have accepted certain duties because of my profession. I have filled offices in the ministerial association, helped establish an emergency telephone referral service, assisted in settling strikes, interceded with county commissioners for changes people felt were needed, designed special programs to foster interfaith cooperation, endured radio interviews for countless causes, spoken to an endless number of groups on a myriad of subjects, and generally run myself into the ground, content that the harder I worked the more God would be pleased.

I now think that a lot of that activity was wasted. It was important, I suppose, but for me to try to do everything was to steal from others the growth that comes when they do things for themselves. Halfway through my present pastorate I went back to school to learn more skills, presumably so that I could work even harder and please God even more. But thanks to the good sense of one particular professor, I discovered that feverish activity by itself does not necessarily move the kingdom forward at all. This was a major step in my spiritual growth. I have finally become content to let the church design its own program and take responsibility for its unique ministry. I serve as a resource, which is what they called me to do in the first place; I let the people run the church. The great benefit is that I can leave at any time without fearing that the whole structure will collapse because it had all been balanced on my back. At first it was humbling to discover that things ran more smoothly this way than when I had attempted to do everything myself. But the members of the church have gained a greater investment in the program, and I have found more time for my family and for writing.

Every church must eventually take responsibility for its own ministry. Each community of believers has a different set of needs, and there is a variety of activities through which the love of Christ can become real to different people. Pastors coming in from the outside do not know at first what the people in the congregation need in order to grow most effectively. If they assume that they do and impose their wills upon the members of the church, they will be violating something essential in the relationship of these people to God.

My first church was a little country parish in Ohio. The church building was an attractive edifice with stained glass windows and a pipe organ. I was very pleased with the facilities except that we had a center pulpit. I had grown up in a church that had a divided chancel and a large walk-in pulpit. I decided we needed these features in this little church. It would open up the chancel area, make possible more flexible programming, enlarge the choir space, and generally make the church more attractive.

Assuming that making the change was my job, I took charge. I drew up the sketches, made a little model of the proposed chancel, and pushed the project through an elders' meeting. When we held a congregational meeting to vote on the remodeling. I argued for the project rather than simply moderating the meeting. When my proposal was approved, I even went so far as to supervise the workers as they did the work according to my specifications. When the project was completed, it was mine, not the congregation's. Then, within two years, I left the church. Why they let me have my way I will never know, except that they loved me and were very tolerant.

I still have friends in that congregation, surprisingly; and whenever I see them, they never fail to remind me that they are still saddled with that monstrosity of a chancel, which I loved so much and which they so despise, and that never a Sunday goes by that they do not think of me with a variety of feelings.

I didn't know what was best for them. I discovered that fact too late to save them the pain. I know now that *my* idea of what will be best for someone usually turns out to be a disaster. Unless programs are matched to the people's needs, unless they are designed to achieve goals that the people themselves have set, and unless the congregation does the actual work, all of our furious activity will not bring the kingdom one day closer.

Evangelism

Evangelism is perhaps *the* most activist behavior of Christians. Evangelism is reaching out into the world to make it Christian as well as to make it better. It is an effort which assumes that to be "Christian" is the most desirable kind of improvement.

The evangelical aspect of the church's work has behind it the command of Christ: "Go, then, to all peoples everywhere and make them my disciples: baptize them . . . and teach them to obey everything I have commanded you" (Matthew 28:19-20). We cannot ignore this command without rejecting Christ's authority, and when we do that we cease to be Christian.

This reaching out—this passionate desire to change the world so that it becomes like heaven, a human kingdom ruled by God—is one of the major strengths of Christianity. This is the high hope promised in a vision in the Revelation: "The kingdom of the world has become the kingdom of our Lord and of his Christ, and he shall reign for ever and ever" (Revelation 11:15, RSV). To bring heaven to earth, to make the world a place where God rules and where God's love is law is a great and glorious goal. It is what we would expect Jesus to require of us;

it is the end toward which we struggle individually and collectively in our local congregations.

Of course we know that because we are human our efforts, even in this area, are distorted by selfishness, pride, and ego. Under the guise of the gospel we have exported nationalism, political power, Western culture, and moral standards that were foreign to those being evangelized. We have been patronizing, thinking that more primitive peoples are not acceptable to God unless they first accept the moral and economic attitudes of those who went to evangelize them. This is not what Jesus had in mind. He mentioned "all peoples everywhere," not limiting them to the industrial powers or English-speaking people or those with Western standards. It is sad to read in the history of mission work how often the early missionaries treated the people among whom they worked with what can only be called contempt—with no appreciation for their own culture, feelings, or ideas. We cannot love people whom we do not respect. The church has finally realized some of its mistakes in this area.

The church does not yet fully realize, however, its continuing error on the local level. Many churches do not have an evangelistic emphasis. Some churches have a reputation for sophistication and propriety in worship because they shy away from the kind of noisy spontaneity often associated with revival services.

A story is told about a man who went into such a church for an evening service. He had grown up in a Pentecostal family, but he had not been to church for many years. He recognized that he was a sinner in need of spiritual help, and he prayed intently during the service that God would touch him. As the preacher delivered the sermon, the man continued to pray that he would be moved by God's Spirit. Finally, full of expectancy, he raised his eyes to heaven and felt the light of God falling on him. In ecstasy, he jumped from his seat, shouting, "Hallelujah! I got religion, I got religion!" The minister stopped, aghast, in midsentence. Shocked by this lack of decorum, he fixed a disapproving look on the man and said, "Well, sit down and be quiet about it. You didn't get it here."

I know how that preacher felt. It's not that one can't "get religion" in this kind of a church, but there is an assumption that any attack of the Spirit that would cause one to make a scene must be "bad" religion. And we don't promote bad religion. So goes the reasoning.

In some of the major denominations, decorum seems to be a priority far ahead of spontaneity. A church school class I was teaching once discussed the various Protestant approaches to worship. A former Pentecostal was in the group. He was the husband of a member of the church but had never joined the congregation himself. He seldom spoke in class, preferring to listen quietly to the discussion. On this occasion we spoke of the differences between mainline denominational and Pentecostal services. Hearing a subject about which he was familiar, he said, "I'll never forget my shock when I first came to this church. It was the first time I had attended a non-Pentecostal church. The biggest surprise was the bulletin. You had everything written down that you were going to do during the service. I could have predicted at 11:00 what you would be doing at 11:45. It seemed to me that everything was so rigid and tightly planned that you didn't leave any room for the Holy Spirit. It was almost as if you were afraid that the Holy Spirit might spring some surprises on you."

Some churches have taken from Paul the phrase "decently and in order" (see 1 Corinthians 14:40, RSV) and have applied it almost as a catch phrase to everything in the church. I have heard countless times, "Now, we must do this decently and in order," or, "You will not be using decency and order if you do that." I agree wholeheartedly with the need for decency, dignity, and planning in the church. It is God's house, and we need to conduct ourselves with decorum when we do God's work. But when we put the need for order and formality ahead of everything else, we lose flexibility, sometimes miss hearing what God is saying, and often quench the Spirit. I am afraid that, for many of us, this is a mask to disguise our lack of commitment, to direct attention away from the faltering fires that burn within us. We shout at football games; we get passionate with our lovers; but we sit in church without emotion because we must be dignified. Nonsense! When God takes hold of us, formality is the least of our concerns.

How can a congregation be made aware of its evangelistic obligation without violating its unique character? Not every person has the same understanding of what is meant by evangelism. How far is far enough, and when do we cross the line into what is inappropriate or even divisive?

Two couples in our congregation had been good friends of our family for years. We had been back and forth to one another's homes and had shared a good deal with each other. They were active in the church, holding various offices, and were always present on Sunday mornings, sitting in front of the pulpit and regularly making helpful and supportive remarks.

Then, suddenly, they "got religion." If it wasn't a bad dose, it was certainly peculiar. It caused them to turn on this church in which they had been happily involved for so many years. They held lengthy and intense conversations with me and with some of the officers. They told me to my face that I wasn't a Christian because I didn't hold an altar

call at the end of the morning service. They began to plan their own
Bible study groups, usually on the book of Revelation; they attempted
to gather around themselves people who agreed that the church was not
doing a proper job. The congregation, interestingly enough, was very
tolerant of their flagrant attempts to cause schism in the church; people
attended these study groups sincerely trying to understand what these
four people, and the outside speakers they brought in, were trying to
say. Many members, however, came away offended by the hostility
and oppressed by the judgmental quality and lack of love that pervaded
these meetings. One of the four told me that the two families were
considering leaving the church. I admit that I had entertained the idea
of their leaving, but I counseled them to stay. "This is your church,"
I told them. "If you have something from God to say to us, we need
to hear it even if it is painful." This went on for some time until they
realized that they were not getting a hearing; finally they joined a
Pentecostal church. To be truthful, we all heaved a sigh of relief because
a very difficult period had come to an end.

Were we not hearing something that God was saying? Were we
running a false church simply because we did not have evangelistic
services? Is the legitimate love and caring we have for one another
something real to God? The lack of love, the hostility, and the divisiveness exhibited by these four did not seem Christlike. Some members
are still troubled by the issue; are we really not doing our job?

There was something important we had to learn from the couples
who left. They were right to say that we should hold before people the
need to make a personal decision to put Christ first in their lives. They
were wrong to do this in an atmosphere of hostility. It became a personal
struggle, a matter of ego, a power clash for control of the church. When
that happens, Jesus Christ is relegated to the back seat. I still don't
know why it happened. A dark shadow hung over the church for months.
These people accused me of working for the devil, even after they had
sat and listened to my preaching for years. I would not reverse the
accusation, but I wonder where the anger and malice they exhibited
came from. Certainly not from Christ.

Our local evangelistic efforts over the years have been along a
different line. We have worked through small groups and have found
a renewal of vitality in the church and a deepening of personal commitment among individual members. This approach has resulted in
more love among members, a greater understanding of what it means
to be "in Christ," and a deeper sense of belonging to the family of
faith. These attributes, in my opinion, mark the program as authentically
evangelistic.

I enjoy working with small groups so much that I am tempted to neglect other aspects of my work so as to have more time for this particular ministry. Troubled about this, I once asked a seminary professor for his opinion. He said, "Your job as pastor is to identify the remnant—that small percentage of the congregation which at any given moment is eager for spiritual growth—and enable them for ministry." That comment was tremendously helpful to me. He was saying that people grow spiritually at different rates and that those who are ripe deserve special attention. This is one criticism of the mass approach to evangelism. In small groups we find those who are ready at the moment for new growth and deeper commitment; people learn and work in a highly intense experience that would not be acceptable to everyone.

In our church, our small group program involves groups of eight people who spend a year sharing things of personal interest. The eight meet with regularity and agree to be present at every meeting so that the group is always intact. The early meetings are spent in creating a sense of trust among the members; so it is possible to share thoughts that members have previously kept to themselves. In the course of learning trust, people lower their defenses and start to say things like "I never told that to anyone before," or "I have known you for years but this is the first time you feel like a real person to me." Eventually, through a number of exercises, people begin to feel an acceptance they have not experienced before. They discover that opening themselves to others is in fact opening themselves to God. This openness does not make people dislike them, as they feared; rather, it allows people to come close, often for the first time. At some point they make a similar discovery about God, that openness to God reveals God's love and acceptance not judgment. This is what makes the small group technique an evangelistic tool. Somewhere in the middle of the process, the Holy Spirit breaks in and the meeting becomes a celebration. The group discovers the spiritual basis of life—relationships, with others and with God—and that is an exquisite moment for them. The members suddenly understand what Christian faith is all about. They understand on a much deeper level what Jesus was saying. They feel the presence of the Spirit, and God becomes real. It is wonderfully exciting. I have seen it happen again and again, and it is always new and joyful. To me, leading people to experience the Good News of Christ in tangible ways is the deep meaning of evangelism. It can happen to those who have been church members for years as well as to those outside the church.

No one method of evangelism works everywhere. Each group needs to find the style that works for it and is consistent with the goals of the church and commands of Christ. It is important to be interested in statistics, to be able to report at the year's end how many conversions have taken place through the work of the congregation. But an emphasis on statistics can cloud the real issue. What is important is not how many people walk to the altar but how many people have actually done some spiritual growing. We need to bring people to Christ, but we also need to deepen their faith once they are in the church. Who is to say which is more important? Each growth spurt can be the equivalent of a new conversion. I can continually remind people that I was converted on January 1, 1943, but if I am always looking backward to that date and have not grown in the meantime, that event is meaningless. I cannot run my car on the gasoline I bought ten years ago. In the same way, I have to be converted again when I am fifty-two because the faith I had when I was ten no longer fits my needs today.

Evangelism means "good news." It asks the question, What does the Good News of God in Christ mean to me at this moment in my life? The question comes to me with a different impact when I am twenty-one, thirty-five, fifty, and eighty. Evangelization is a process, not an event. The church truly interested in evangelism needs to address this fact, to make certain that it is not simply doing the same thing over and over again. Most of all, evangelism means growth.

Special Ministries

Another form of Activist Christianity is the establishment of special ministries aimed at groups with particular needs and operated in the name of Christ.

Alcoholics Anonymous meets in our church, as does Al-Anon, a related group for family members of alcoholics. A downtown church sponsors a "Creative Divorce" group. Another has developed a ministry to retired people that includes a recreation center with a full-time director. A black minister is administrator of a community center in a poorer section of town; this center helps people gain their rights, improve their circumstances, and participate in remedial classes to upgrade their skills. Church-based inner-city programs of this nature are common nowadays and take seriously the comment of Christ, "Whenever you did this for one of the least important of these brothers of mine, you did it for me" (Matthew 25:40). If we don't export our faith into the communities in which we live and care for those whom the world seems to have ignored or crushed and then forgotten, how will the kingdom come? The Christian church has been noted for special programs of compassion across the years, ministries in which the "Word has become flesh." Hospitals, homes for the aged, children's homes, prison ministries, homes for unwed mothers—all of these and countless other imaginative ways of helping people began because the compassion of Christ took root in the lives of some of his followers. People knew that they had to do more than talk about Christ's compassion within the four walls of their churches on Sunday mornings.

Six other ministers and I helped set up an emergency counseling and intervention telephone service in our community some years ago. It has become a large, well-organized program staffed by a full-time administrator and scores of trained volunteers. But in those early days we were operating from day to day and our future seemed precarious. Each of the seven ministers had a special phone by the bed; and we took turns answering it one night a week. During the day, calls were handled by a local mental health agency.

Many a night I would answer the phone at 3:30 A.M. or so, while my long-suffering wife pulled the pillow over her head or gave up altogether and went to sleep on the sofa. I recall talking to a potential suicide one night while my wife was asleep in the living room; the bedroom door was closed. I decided to have the call traced, but I didn't want the person on the phone to know what I was doing. It became obvious that I needed my wife's help. Not being able to call her, I began throwing shoes—and anything else I could lay my hands on in the dark—at the bedroom door until the racket finally brought her in, a curious expression on her face. She called the police on our own phone, and the intervention was made. This was only one of many incidents which proved that although it completely disrupted our lives, the service was a worthwhile thing for the churches to be doing.

One of the exciting things for a church to do is to decide in what unique and personal way it will translate into action Christ's command to care for the needy. Each congregation has something distinctive to offer to the church's overall ministry.

A member of one local church felt that God was leading her to initiate a deaf ministry in her church. The church had no deaf members, and no one in the congregation knew sign language. Nevertheless, she coordinated a project in which a number of people were trained to interpret for the deaf during church services, Bible studies, and other programs. When it was announced that they were ready to begin, deaf people came forward whom no one had known about before; these people had never been able to benefit from church participation because of their deafness. The program now helps a large number of people from the entire community, because one person saw a need and followed the Holy Spirit's leading.

These ministries of compassion are the church outside its own walls.

It is this kind of work to which Christ leads us when he says, "Follow me."

Justice

Working for human justice is another area of Activist Christianity. The civil rights marches of the last decades were classic examples. There was so much activism in the churches during the 1960s and 1970s, however, that an inevitable reaction set in. A great many people, especially those who hold the Traditional position, object to the church's "running around meddling in everybody's business." One of the most common questions heard during that period was "Why can't the church just stick to the simple gospel?" It was difficult to convince people that the gospel constrained us to do precisely these things—to care for the downtrodden, to set the captives at liberty—to follow the example of Jesus who came specifically to preach Good News to hopeless people. The fact is that the church did not come near to doing its job in the recent past. If it had been faithful to the gospel commands, it would have produced so many Christians actively clamoring for justice that there would have been a civil rights revolution. But the church was timid, as usual, and only isolated individuals took up the challenge. Of course the church is also responsible to the many who are afraid of the gospel's call to the Activist life. How do we obey Christ and still minister to those who are wary of change? That is a tension the church has always faced.

I once preached a sermon that took a stand against capital punishment. I didn't think it was a particularly daring thing to do because I was firmly convinced that executions were wrong on New Testament grounds. As a result, I did not expect any serious disagreement. I was mistaken. I live in a strongly law-and-order area, where people not only have a deep-seated need to see wrongdoers punished but also justify their beliefs by referring to certain passages in the Bible, particularly in the Old Testament. One lawyer in the congregation, who believed that capital punishment was the keystone of the whole criminal justice system, was so angered by the sermon that he left the church. When I asked him why he had reacted in such a way, he told me that I had misused the pulpit. I had taken one point of view; I had not given a balanced presentation of a topic that has two sides; and I had not allowed any comments from those who disagreed with me. He was right. I was so convinced of my own position that I had made no allowance for the position of others. I should have either presented both sides or brought the subject up in another setting where there could have been general discussion. I am still convinced that my position is right, but I communicated it in the wrong way, forcing those who disagreed to sit silently and listen. That is not the way to convince anyone of anything, a fact we need to remember when we are tempted to get carried away with a favorite cause.

There are innumerable reasons for Christians to get involved in the cause of justice: to help those whom no one else cares to help, to seek the very people to whom Jesus came to minister, to love them in his name, and to remind ourselves that all people everywhere are God's children, equally deserving of respect and care.

Many people do not think that this is the church's business, or they prefer to use their money and energy in different ways. When this is so, however, it becomes apparent that our form of Christianity is not out to change the world but to resist change at all costs, primarily for our own selfish benefit. It is interesting to note that where people are comfortable and in control of the sources of power, Christianity is often deployed to maintain their rights and privileges. When the people have been repressed and have been denied their rights, then their faith becomes a rallying point, the moral focus behind their efforts to gain their rightful powers and privileges. That fact says that we can use our faith to suit our own purposes rather than letting God use us. We do not listen to what the gospel really says; we make it say what we want to hear so that we can continue doing what we want to do. That, of course, is a perversion. Those who do not think that Christianity has work to do in the world had better go back and read their New Testament. Those who would use it as a revolutionary tool that encourages violence and brutality in the quest for what they call freedom had better go back and read their New Testament also.

The Traditional position teaches us what is of value from the past, while the Authoritarian position gives us the structure of the faith we preach. But if we do not go out actively into the world to put these truths into action, if the Word that shines through us does not take on our flesh, then we have missed the essential teaching of Jesus. He did not say, "Sit in church." Nor did he say, "Study your Bible." He said, "Go into all the world" (Mark 16:15, RSV). Our enthusiasm to obey not only will demonstrate the depth of our commitment but also will help determine whether the kingdom will be early or late in coming.

5

The Transcendent Position

A group from our church once attended a three-day conference to learn how to develop leadership for a small-groups ministry. We had been getting increasingly excited about these groups that were just taking hold in our church; we had seen people touched and their lives changed for the better through this approach. As a result we wanted as much information about this form of ministry as possible.

I was pleased that three men and seven women were willing to take three days off from work so they could attend the conference. The ten of us joined people from other churches in town, and we all traveled together in an old bus that two of the churches had purchased jointly. The bus was painted in psychedelic colors and did not work very well, so using it was an act of faith as well as a test of our self-confidence. We left feeling full of anticipation.

For three days we got to know new people and experienced in a fresh way what it meant to be a family of faith. Since the people from our church were separated during the day (having become members of different "families" at the conference), we spent a great deal of each evening (and sometimes part of the night) crammed into one of our hotel rooms, comparing notes, debriefing, and enjoying being together.

The trip home was an ecstatic party. Our laughing, singing, and sharing of experiences from the conference reflected a joyous mood that matched the colors of the bus. When we got home, the enthusiasm, instead of dying, burned hotter. We were frequently on the phone to one another, or in one another's homes, talking about the trip, planning how to involve the congregation in small-group work, preparing to introduce this ministry on the following Sunday, and basking in a continuation of joyful feelings that none of us understood but hoped would never end.

Before the Sunday service, we met in the library almost spontaneously and, holding hands, prayed for the service and the sermon. I went into that service with a fire blazing in me, which spread out to the congregation. That Sunday marked the moment when the whole church moved to a new spiritual level in its life. I pronounced the benediction and, as I was walking down the aisle, the president of the trustees, one of the men who had attended the conference, jumped out of his pew enthusiastically and hugged me in full view of the congregation.

Now, let me assure you that we are typical, conservative, undemonstrative Christians. These things do not usually happen among us. We believe in decency and order. At least, we always had, but as we met during the next week to tighten our plans and reflect on the Sunday service, someone asked, "What's going on? What has happened to us?" In the silence that followed, someone speculated, "I think it's the Holy Spirit. I think the power of the Spirit has touched us."

I shall never forget hearing those words. It sounds funny to say now; the work of the Spirit has become familiar and eagerly sought among us, but at that moment the idea fell on us like a blow from a hammer, a shock that stunned us into silence. We were educated, mainline, Protestant Christians! We didn't fool around with the Holy Spirit. That was for Pentecostals and other churches who didn't care about dignity and decorum. All of our prejudices surfaced in that moment. We reviewed silently all the times we had ignored or made fun of others who had been carried away by the Spirit. This was something we had been programmed to distrust and reject. Surely this could not be happening to us. If it were true, nothing would ever be the same again.

All of these thoughts passed through our minds in an instant and just as quickly were dismissed. One person spoke up and said, "If this is the Holy Spirit, I want all I can get!"

What a revelation! What a glimpse of the light of God! It was a blazing, glorious look into the kingdom, which brought with it an immediate knowledge that Christianity is a joyful, uplifting, daily experience that makes one want to talk about what Jesus Christ is doing in his or her life. In that moment some of our people changed from being exclusively Traditional Christians and began to explore what it means to be a Transcendent Christian.

We made mistakes, of course, as we learned what we were doing. We assumed that the whole congregation was as excited as we were, and almost scared some people out of the church by our excess of zeal. We learned that it is important to take people where they are and to grow with them slowly, so that the work of the Spirit has time to take root.

Those who take the Transcendent position are often so full of their

own personal experience, their own knowledge of the reality and goodness of God, that they sometimes find it hard to identify with those
who are not in the same place. The attitude of those in the Transcendent
position can appear to be condescending—"I have the Spirit and you
don't, and therefore you are obviously lacking something." The Holy
Spirit generates such enthusiasm and joy in people that it is difficult,
especially at first, to avoid this elitist attitude. But as we grow, we
come to a point where we think, not of ourselves and our own experience, but of the needs and feelings of those to whom we are trying
to minister by the power of the Holy Spirit.

The Transcendent position is that experience of faith bounded on the
one hand by the spiritual—concentrating on the things of heaven rather
than the things of earth—and on the other by grace—emphasizing the
love, power, and acceptance of God. Because of this, the stress is not
on what we should do, as in the Authoritarian position, but on all the
possibilities that a loving God holds open to us if we trust and follow
where we are led.

The Transcendent position is characterized by personal religion, meditation and prayer, and charismatic gifts, among other things. We will
also discuss the Electronic Church under this heading.

Personal Religion

As we got further into our small-groups ministry, we discovered the
meaning of the first aspect of the Transcendent position—personal
religion. This is not to say that few people had had a close personal
relationship with Christ before this happened. Rather, it means that we
often did not know how to give these people opportunities to share their
faith; we did not surround them with an environment that would help
them grow spiritually. Call it prejudice if you like, but we, like many
others, had been put off by the "fanatic fringe," who could talk about
nothing except being born again, who were always standing on street
corners accosting strangers with the question "Are you saved, brother?"
To many of us it didn't seem possible to be saved and sane at the same
time. We believed that faith is a private thing and should be kept to
oneself; at least, this is what we had been taught.

The question raised by the two couples who left the church because
we didn't end our services with an altar call was a real one. How do
we obey the command of Christ to be courageous about proclaiming
our faith and yet respect the basic sensibilities of those involved? Is the
sawdust trail the only path along which to walk in the pursuit of spiritual
growth? Does one have to end up looking like an unsophisticated
religious fanatic in order to take Christ seriously? We discovered that

the answer is no. There is a pathway that is appropriate for each person, a pathway that takes into account one's background and specific needs and that offers an outlet for Christian expression that does not force one to compromise personal style. My view is that each individual and each church can find the paths that best suit them only by experimentation and experience.

We soon had prayer groups, spiritual-growth groups, and a number of ways in which people could share in specific detail what Jesus Christ was doing in their lives at the moment. These groups enabled people to talk about their personal struggles and to be encouraged by the support of others. This sharing became a source of sustenance for those involved so that they eagerly looked forward to the meetings. Where else, they asked, was it possible to talk about urgent and personal matters with people who understood and cared?

Our sharing also changed the way some of us approached others. A woman sat in my study one day, not long after this had all begun. She was the picture of failure and depression. She said she was at the bottom of her life: she was an alcoholic; her second marriage was failing; she was hopeless and ready to quit. She had tried everything, she told me, and nothing had worked. What could she do?

I looked at her for a long time. I didn't know the woman or anything about her except what she had just told me. After I had listened to her for most of an hour, I said, "It sounds as though you need a relationship with Christ." A natural thing for a Christian minister to say to a suffering person? Not necessarily. That had not been my style. I had recently completed a master's degree in counseling and had begun to be swamped by requests for counseling from all over the community. My normal approach would have been to treat this problem from its psychological aspects and let the faith end of the matter take care of itself. After all, her faith was ultimately a personal thing. Quite frankly, I was not brought up in a tradition that confronted people in such a bold, spiritual way.

But as I looked at that woman, sitting defeated in my study, I knew she needed Christ. It was such a clear revelation that other considerations were unimportant. It was a Holy Spirit insight, and it was the Holy Spirit who gave me power to say the words, beginning an approach I had never used before.

She sat there and looked at me, her eyes wide in thought. After a long moment she said in a tiny and somewhat surprised voice, "You're right!" We finished our talk and she went home. A few days later, she was back again, totally transformed. Her face was shining. She could not stop smiling. Everything she said was full of enthusiasm, and I could sense the utter sincerity in every word she spoke. Her life had gained an entirely new perspective. It was the Spirit who had directed our encounter that first day, and it was the Spirit who was now motivating the change in her. In a strange way, I sat outside the experience. I knew I had not been responsible for this change by my masterful use of psychological theory and technique. That would have taken months. Rather, I had been a channel through which the Spirit had quite simply worked a miracle—and in only two days!

In the weeks that followed, the woman stopped drinking; her changed attitude ended the troubles at home about which she had been complaining. Her husband could not believe that all this was really happening. The only thing she wanted to talk about in our sessions was Jesus Christ and what he was doing in her life. Life suddenly had a holy meaning for her, and that meaning focused on Christ. "He's my best friend, my very best friend," I heard her repeat over and over again. Today, years later, she has lost none of her enthusiasm for the spiritual miracle that changed her completely.

That experience was also responsible for a great leap forward in my own spiritual growth; I learned to trust the Spirit to do the leading and the healing. Not that I stopped using my psychological training in working with people, but it now became obvious that spiritual therapy is also a legitimate and effective tool. In fact, it is the most important tool, for if the Spirit is not the therapist, then we who counsel do so in vain.

The theme of this book is balance, finding the part of the truth that each group has to offer and avoiding the extremes on either end that lead to distortion. If we were to generalize, we might say that the primary objection that the mainline churches have against the evangelicals is their preoccupation with conversion, as though a single historic personal decision is all that is required to make one a Christian, even though there often seems to be no growth beyond that point. But the evangelical counterobjection is that the mainline churches are forever talking about nurture, Christian education, and growth for those who are already Christians, without ever confronting people with the need to make a personal decision for Christ. This is a generalization but, insofar as it is true, it demonstrates that each group tends to focus on different halves of the Christian experience. Evangelism ought to result in the salvation of the whole person, but we often split the experience down the middle. The evangelicals concentrate on the spiritual needs of the person and minimize physical needs. At the other extreme, many mainline churches shy away from talking about the spiritual person but spend a great deal of time asking how the Christian, once converted, is supposed to deal with the world. We need to see that these concerns are complementary—halves of the same issue; one approach by itself is incomplete. Both groups can teach the other in this area if they are both willing to listen.

Perhaps the truest insight into the matter came to us one day after we had been exploring the Spirit's work for a number of months. People looked forward to the group meetings; we found strength in sharing our trials and victories; and we were excited to discover that the Spirit really gave us answers and provided recognizable direction. As we sought God's purpose for our lives, our desire to share our discoveries increased so that we often talked about how to reach out to others with the claims of a personal God. After one such discussion, a member suddenly said, "You know, we sound like those so-called 'religious nuts' we once avoided. Maybe this is what they were feeling all along. Maybe we just never understood."

Meditation and Prayer

Communication with God through meditation and prayer is another great aspect of Transcendent Christianity. There are all sorts of references in Scripture that point to the need for quiet time alone with God. Jesus spent a great deal of time meditating in lonely places so that he could keep his relationship with God intimate and filled with power. Private times with God are major sources of strength for Christians, and we neglect them at great cost to ourselves.

Some years ago I became interested in the meditation movement that was then in vogue—Transcendental Meditation ("T. M."). Twice a day I sat in silence, repeating my mantra and learning to clear my mind so that I could transcend the world and become one with the Infinite. I had only partial success. I learned to relax and received some useful ideas for writing and for other projects, but for the most part I never saw "the light."

Some people, however, thought I was definitely plunging into darkness. My meditating was one of the reasons the two couples (to whom I referred earlier) left the church; they were convinced that I was consorting with the devil. They thought that I was dallying with pagan practices; they were certain that it was unchristian for someone who stood in the pulpit regularly and told others how to live the Christian life to engage in meditation.

I found in time that "T. M." did not meet my needs. It succeeded in teaching me to become silent and touch my inner resources. Later I discovered writers who suggest how these disciplines can be used within a Christian framework. I also developed a technique of my own that involves visualizing an encounter with Christ and listening to what he has to say on a particular day about a specific concern. It is surprising how clearly Christ can speak when one takes time to listen. At other times, I use the name "Jesus" as a mantra, repeating it over and over in an attempt to sense his presence in me, filling me, guiding me.

Most people find it difficult to deal with silence. If there are thirty seconds of silence during worship, most congregations get a bad case of the fidgets. But if we never come silently before God, waiting, listening, and willing to be guided, how can we say that we are disciples of Christ? Disciples are those who learn from someone, and Christ is our teacher. He asks us, "Why do you call me, 'Lord, Lord' and yet don't do what I tell you?" (Luke 6:46). How can we *do* what he says if we do not *listen* to what he says? If prayer is talking to God, then meditation is listening for the answer. The two go together. Many of us err in not praying regularly, but most of us make the mistake of thinking we can pray without meditating. We are good at telling God what we want but lacking in our willingness to listen to what God wants from us. Meditation is one of the most intimate personal experiences of faith. It is an ongoing confession that we want God to be real to us, that we want God to live in us and help us be aware of God's presence at all times. These are profound ideas, and we cannot express them more sincerely than in regular meditation. If, as the woman in my study said, "Jesus is my best friend," then we should want to spend time with God, whether we visualize the eternal Father or the incarnate Son, or both. If we cannot find the time for that, then we are fooling ourselves about that supposed friendship.

Our church tried an interesting experiment one Christmas season. Some of us had been complaining about how busy we were during Advent and how rushed our schedules were, both at home and in the church, so that we had little time to experience the real meaning of the season. These are common complaints, and we had heard them before. But this year we decided to do something about the matter. We planned a meditative pre-Advent retreat, an all-day affair at the church. About a dozen people came and we spent seven hours together from 9 A.M. until 4 P.M.

The emphasis was on time alone in private prayer and meditation. We outlined a number of Scripture passages that contrasted the light of the gospel with the darkness of the world. We suggested that the participants list what had made them unhappy about previous Christmas seasons as a way of improving things this year. We itemized things to pray for and then learned methods of meditative prayer. From time to time we came together to discuss what was happening.

For about half the day each participant was alone in a private spot in the church. Three and a half hours of silence in one day was quite a bit for people who had had no experience in meditation, and they expected the time to drag interminably. Without exception, they were amazed at how quickly the time went. They discovered that it took time for their internal clocks to slow down, but that when this happened, the time went faster and God seemed to become more real. In the process, they felt a deep sense of peace, which was totally unexpected.

After Christmas, most of them reported that the calmness had continued through the season, that they had been less rushed and distracted, and that they had had more time to experience what was happening. Most of all, they discovered that Christ was at the center of everything they did, making the whole season more meaningful and the time spent with their families more uplifting. That was quite an accomplishment for people unfamiliar with such a discipline. It is a testimony to the power of prayer and meditation to produce long-term results.

A daily time of talking with God in prayer and listening for God's response in meditation is one of the chief disciplines of the Transcendent aspect of Christianity. It is making concrete the urgent spiritual desire to "become one with the Infinite."

Charismatic Gifts

There can be no doubt that we are in the midst of a Holy Spirit revival throughout the church. This is the reason we are hearing so much these days about charismatic faith and the gifts of the Spirit, a third aspect of the Transcendent position. To those who find a personal relationship with Christ and then seek a closer walk with God through meditation and prayer, there sometimes come special gifts, or charismata, which God intends them to use for the upbuilding of the church and for the blessing of people. But charismatics have often been badly misunderstood by those in the mainline denominations. Because of their talk about healing, speaking in tongues, and other ecstatic forms of religious behavior, they are often given wide berth by those who are interested in a moderate and intellectual approach to Christian faith.

This is unfortunate and is simply one more form of prejudice. Paul talks at length in 1 Corinthians 12 about the gifts of the Spirit, suggesting that God has given us a variety of ways to serve one another and that therefore we need one another. He tells us, "There are different kinds of spiritual gifts, but the same Spirit gives them." He goes on to say that the Spirit's presence is shown in some way in every person who uses his or her particular spiritual gift and that this individual gift is for the good of all. Then he lists the gifts: messages full of wisdom, messages full of knowledge, faith, the power to heal, the power to work miracles, the ability to speak God's message, the ability to discern which gifts come from God and which do not, the ability to speak in tongues and to interpret messages in tongues. Paul repeats at the end of the passage that "it is one and the same Spirit who does all this; as he wishes, he gives a different gift to each person."

Not everyone has all the gifts: ". . . not all [are] apostles or prophets or teachers. Not everyone has the power to work miracles or to heal diseases or to speak in strange tongues or to explain what is said." Since not everyone has all the gifts, the church needs all people working together in order to have the full range of gifts at its disposal. Therefore, we are not to despise those who have different gifts from ours, because we need their gifts as much as they need ours.

Because not everyone has every gift, we would think that those who possess a special gift would be among the spiritual elite. Our supply-and-demand culture teaches us that if a commodity is in short supply, the one who possesses it is in a stronger position than others. Not so with the gifts of the Spirit. Paul says exactly the opposite. Since not all are prophets or teachers or healers, these gifts cannot be the most important. They cannot be required for entrance into the kingdom, or they would have been given to everyone. So Paul says, in effect, that since God has chosen not to give these gifts to everyone, we should set our hearts on the more important gifts. The most important of all the gifts is love, the one gift that is required of everyone.

So the gifts possessed by a few—healing, speaking in tongues, leadership—although they are important to the church, are the less important gifts. Those who work with these gifts, while doing an important and necessary work for God, need not feel puffed up and superior. They have been singled out not so much to receive special honor as to perform a special chore within the church. The attitude of elitism, a preoccupation with the gift for its own sake and the tendency to exalt oneself rather than God, who gave the gift, has turned many away from the charismatic experience. Paul puts healing, helping others, directing them, and speaking in strange tongues at the bottom of the list, following apostles, prophets, teachers, and miracle workers (see 1 Corinthians 12:28). In the highest place of all he puts those who love. Since all of these are gifts, we cannot boast about our possession of them. We did not earn them; having them brings us no credit. Rather, their appearance in our lives demands extra work of us.

Those who do not consider themselves charismatic should dwell on this passage from Paul. If we are truly followers of Christ and if we seek in prayer to be more like him, then the love that shows through us is the love of Christ, not something we have generated by our own energy and goodness. It is given to us by the grace of God through the power of the Holy Spirit. This makes our "gift" the gift of love; therefore, in the truest sense, we are charismatic, exhibiting in our lives the most important of all the gifts of the Holy Spirit. If we use the term "charismatic" to refer only to those who display the more dramatic gifts, we have completely missed Paul's meaning. Surely this is something for mainline Christians, and for all who have a prejudice against the more exuberant expressions of the faith, to consider.

Yet, a gift is a gift. It is not asked for; it is given. Sometimes it comes as a total surprise.

Betty, a woman in our congregation, has belonged to the church for years. She has done all the traditional lay leadership jobs but was never verbal about her personal faith. Then several years ago her husband died suddenly. (He was the trustee who jumped into the aisle and hugged me on that memorable Sunday morning.) Betty was left with three boys to raise, and the shock was overwhelming. She spent months being angry with God as she searched helplessly for a way to pull herself back into life.

Then things began to happen. People in prayer groups outside our church began to pray for her. Women in charismatic organizations invited her to meetings, and she began to be cared for in tangible and helpful ways by those who represented a different style of faith from the one to which she had been accustomed. Gradually, she began to change. She wasn't being wooed away from the church. She stayed active and involved in the congregation's work but began to add new dimensions to her faith. She would often attend our worship service in the morning and a charismatic "Prayer and Praise" service elsewhere in the evening. She went away to conferences on the work of the Holy Spirit, and we witnessed a dynamic new quality of faith surfacing in her life. She had always been an average churchgoer, quiet about her religious life and not anxious to share the details of her spiritual growth. Then all that changed. She formed study groups in the church and sat in on those led by others. In these groups she spoke simply and movingly about what was happening to her. She described how God had become real in her life, how her new and broader outlook on personal faith had become intensely exciting for her. She made no attempt to force her new ideas on anyone; she simply witnessed quietly to the changes God was making in her life. People who had known her before she became a widow, especially those who remembered her pain during those first lonely months of anger and rebellion, were amazed at what they saw. Betty was a different woman.

And then she was given the gift of healing. People in the congregation, who had never before had in their midst anyone who possessed one of the more dramatic gifts, were astonished; they still speak of her as "our resident charismatic." She didn't ask for the gift; she didn't even want it. In fact, at first she tried to pretend that it hadn't happened. I remind you, we were not experienced at this sort of thing; we had always believed that this form of religious expression was best left to others. At first she didn't know what to do with her gift, but there it was. She had it. There was no question about it. The power would come to her at odd moments in unexpected places, and she would recognize it by the feeling of warmth in her hands. When she laid those hands on the sick and prayed for them, healing took place—not always, but often enough so that we knew she was being used by God. She even had the ability to touch people and sense where their pain was, before they described it in words.

Betty and I attended a retreat with about thirty members of the congregation some months later. During the weekend, one of the people there, a young woman named Nikki, sprained her ankle badly. It caused her severe pain and was so badly swollen that she was barely able to get around the conference grounds. She had to hold onto others to get from one place to another.

After the final service, which ended with Communion, everyone left to climb the hill to the dining hall. Nikki's husband, Ray, went to get the car because he was certain that she would not be able to walk up the hill. Betty waited until everyone was gone and then, timidly, half uncertain of the gift and half afraid of how Nikki would react, asked if she could pray for healing for the ankle. Not many minutes later someone ran up the hill, met Ray who was starting down with the car, and told him to wait. Several moments passed, and then Nikki appeared, walking on the ankle that had given her such pain all weekend. She had a broad smile on her face; the swelling was gone, and the ankle was completely free of pain. Needless to say, there was a lot of discussion among those at the retreat who had heard of such things but had never seen them before.

Gifts are part of the church. We cannot deny or ignore them. We cannot leave them for others to do because the Spirit gives a different gift to each person. If we do not receive one of the more spectacular gifts, we know that we have the most important gift of all, the one required of each one of us, the gift of love. We are all called to be charismatic persons, to receive and use for the upbuilding of the church the good gifts that the Holy Spirit in grace and wisdom decides to give us.

The Electronic Church

I want to refer to the "electronic church" under the heading of the Transcendent position because it fits into the section bounded by grace (a free view of the Christian faith having no relation to denominational law or authority) and the spiritual (a direct personal relationship with God having no connection to the activities of the institutional church.)

There can be no question that televised religion has reached people who would never have responded to the institutional church. A television religious program can be seen in privacy, without obligation or commitment on the part of the viewer. Many people watch it initially because they do not want to walk around the corner to attend an 11 A.M. service. After a program has touched them effectively and brought them into relationship with Christ, some have sought membership in a local church and become active and contributing members. The "electronic church" can reach many who might never be touched by the program of the little church around the corner.

While TV evangelism has great potential for good, the concerned observer cannot help being disappointed by how far short of that potential it has fallen. For one thing, the tremendous diversity of theology and practice within the church is not reflected in the bulk of the religious fare offered. Most of it is evangelical or pentecostal, leaving a large percentage of Christians hungering for programming more suited to their taste. Where are the mainline denominations, the great cathedral services, the current preachers about whom we will be reading generations from now?

The answer is that these expressions of religion do not make exciting television. Those who have a deep desire to share a responsible gospel with a needy world cannot afford to compete with those who hype their message to grab the attention of the bored viewer. The result is that the field is too often left to religious entrepreneurs who cannot distinguish between gospel and ratings and who end up calling more attention to themselves than to the Christ they profess to proclaim. The inevitable consequence is a thin gruel of faith that does not deliver the spiritual nourishment it promises and that too frequently panders to the religious fears of its viewers.

John Killinger has written of the effect upon viewers of such religious television programs:

> TV Christianity is producing a generation of believers whose view of life is so distorted that they do not know how to cope with the simple realities of human existence. They have almost no grasp of the great suffering necessary to overcome the injustices in society. Their Jesus is a plastic Jesus with no real wounds, no crown of thorns, no horrible cross on his

back. He is an antiseptic little Jesus huckstered like cars and laxatives and deodorant soaps, without enough real gospel, as a British preacher once put it, to save a titmouse.[1]

Religious television has many positive aspects, of course, and it needs to deepen its sense of responsibility, not only to the public but most of all to God. Television, however, by its very nature, draws us into a world of imaginative unreality. It paints images that lift us above our routine; it holds up ideals that our daily life cannot match. As a result, it widens the gap between the religion shown on the screen and the religion we experience.

One of the features of the world of televised religion is a large production budget that makes possible all sorts of varied and stimulating presentations. We see what the gospel is doing on the other side of the world; we hear people talk about their miraculous experiences of the grace of God; we see mass healing services; and we witness the power of the Spirit doing astounding things that bring praise flooding spontaneously from us. To a great extent, however, these presentations make the local church program look dull and drab by comparison, much as *Sesame Street* does for the local kindergarten. So, while such programs may stimulate us, inspire us, and create high moments of faith for us individually, they may cut us off to a degree from the real world. I sometimes have the same reaction to a good motion picture. I get completely engrossed in it, carried away for a moment into a world larger than my world. Then there is a disappointing moment when the houselights come on and I have to walk back into the dark, unromantic world, realizing that the make-believe world in which I had been so involved does not really exist.

The exciting world portrayed by the electronic church may exist, but it is not my world. When I shut the set off, I have to deal with real people, not all of whom are as full of faith and joy as those I have seen on the tube. I have to go to a church where the program is not as spectacular and the speakers not as dynamic as those on television. I have to live in a world where not all the problems are overcome as dramatically as those in the programs I watch. All of this, while it may lift me to wonderful heights, also has the possibility of dashing me to the depths of depression. How do I make a connection between the glorious truths portrayed by the electronic church and the real world of home and church in which I must live from day to day?

Once again, I have to learn that any fragment of the picture by itself is a distortion. In the same way that Jesus would not let Peter, James and John stay on the Mount of Transfiguration but forced them to go back into the dark valley of frustration to share the kingdom with those who had not been to the mountaintop, so we are required to take the inspiration of televised religion and translate it into action where we live. We need to remember the basic truth of the incarnation, that Jesus became flesh because the physical part of creation is an important element in God's plan. We have been commissioned to live in the physical world and deal with hurting, needy, flesh-and-blood people, and this is as important as our desire to escape into the personal world of spiritual encounters with Christ. I do not meet Jesus only in prayer and meditation. I also encounter him in the lives of the people with whom I share high moments of spiritual insight. The gifts of inspiration and exaltation, whether received from television or elsewhere, are not given to me just for my own private enjoyment. They are given so that I can translate that hope and that beauty into spiritual reality in the lives of people without hope and beauty. Thus, the high moments I experience on television should be another commissioning, a demand for added service.

A cartoon on this subject shows a family sitting in the living room in front of the television set. They are dressed casually, and some are even in pajamas. The program they are watching is a religious service and the father, thinking of the advantages of this system, says, "We don't have to get dressed and our church offerings make the payments on the television set!"[2] It is important that televised religion not seduce us into a gospel without responsibility. The gospel message is that I have been bought with a price. Therefore, I cannot accept the gift of salvation without somehow showing my appreciation for what it cost. I am obliged to pass on my knowledge of salvation. The electronic church makes it possible for me to call the phone number on the screen and talk with someone for a moment, but that is not the same thing as being part of an ongoing relationship with a neighbor down the street. It is easy to be on our good behavior during courtship when we are trying to impress someone, but to live peacefully and lovingly in the marriage relationship through all the events of half a century is the real test of strength and commitment. In the same way, it is one thing to think high thoughts about what it means to be a Christian while I am sitting in front of the screen and quite another to live out the meaning of that discipleship in the context of a spouse, children, bills, and a church with a thousand fellow members, all of whom see reality somewhat differently than I. It may be from the television program that I get my basic inspiration, but it is in the context of the family of faith that my salvation is worked out day by day, step by tedious step. The statement in Hebrews 10:25 is still relevant in a day of electronic marvels: "Let us not give up the habit of meeting together, as some are doing. Instead, let us encourage one another all the more, since you see that the Day of the Lord is coming nearer.''

The Transcendent position is perhaps the most difficult of the four positions to define and yet, without it, the others lack something essential. The other three will serve no ultimate purpose if those who hold to them are not deeply, personally committed to Jesus Christ. We are not saved, in the final analysis, by our membership in the church, nor by our agreement to an authoritative statement of Christian belief, nor by our busyness in a world that desperately needs to see faith at work. We are saved because of our faith in a living, transcendent Christ and by our personal response to him. For each person that response is different, but for each person there must be some response. God wants to become the living Lord of each life. Of course, we have been put in the world because God wants us to descend from our Transcendent experience to share God's glory with the world. I had a professor who spoke of people who were ''so heavenly-minded that they were no earthly good.'' The Transcendent must express itself through tradition, authority, and the needs of others, or it becomes a selfish and isolated experience. But until we have met the risen Christ on the mountaintop, we have missed a basic part of what it means to be Christian.

6

Moving Through the Positions

Twenty years after I graduated from seminary, I completed a master's degree in what was called "Advanced Pastoral Studies." As a final requirement, I had to write a thesis on a topic of special interest to me. I had always felt a strong negative reaction to prejudice and to prejudiced people. Growing up in an environment that did not allow much contact between people of different races or religions, I had been surrounded by an attitude that held that "our kind doesn't mix with their kind." I do not know where my resistance to that kind of thinking began, but from an early age I knew it was wrong. I was particularly upset by religious prejudice. I decided to use that as the topic for my paper.

The thesis I wanted to test was: "Fundamentalist pastors are by nature prejudiced, thinking themselves superior to, and looking down upon, those with different religious views." I wanted to go to the heart of the issue by dealing with those I felt to be most guilty of religious prejudice. I interviewed fifteen fundamentalist-type pastors and asked them a number of questions designed to help me learn two things about them: how much religious prejudice.did they exhibit and what was its source in their spiritual formation? When I summarized my results, I was in for a terrible shock.

What I discovered in my study of religious prejudice was my own prejudice! That was the last thing I was looking for. I had thought I was the perfectly unprejudiced person, but my paper revealed the dark shadows in my own thinking.

Almost without exception, I was received warmly by these people and ended up making friendships that remain to this day. The pastors were more than willing to talk about their faith and took pleasure in telling me how Christ had become real to them. Because I asked about these deep matters of the soul and listened attentively, they felt a close relationship to me. That encounter broke down the external barriers that had previously kept us apart and united us in a mutual experience of faith. As a result, we discovered a oneness that surprised me and made me take a new look at some of my own ideas about faith. In many ways they became my teachers as well as my brothers in the faith.

What I had expected to find were shallow people who had not thought through the essential aspects of the faith, who were using God to make themselves feel important and to gain authority over others. That prejudice was so deeply ingrained in me that I did not see it as prejudice; to me, it was fact. To be sure, I found some prejudice in their thinking, especially on certain topics such as the ordination of women. One man said that since God had once used a jackass to accomplish his will, he supposed that God would also be able to use women, although he didn't think it was a particularly useful idea. But for the most part, my thesis was shattered by the very people I expected to confirm it. They were loving, caring, deeply spiritual people who were sincerely disturbed by the negative views often held about them by mainline Christians. I concluded the project with great respect for them. Thus, to a certain extent, I became the subject of my own study about prejudice. I am still humbled and troubled about that discovery. If I, who was actively attempting to be unprejudiced in my thinking, could be guilty of harboring such blind spots, does that mean that we are all guilty in one way or another?

The first broad outlines of this book began to take shape in the middle of 1979, and about that time I shared the basic premise with an adult class I have taught for almost twenty years. I presented the ideas in the following way, although here I am exaggerating for effect:

The Traditional position is held by those who see Christianity in organizational terms, who may have conviction about their beliefs but little spirit, whose behavior is characterized by routine and primarily social activities, and who therefore find no joy and little fulfillment in their faith.

People who hold the Authoritarian position see theology as most important, tend to be separatist and to demand conformity; as a result their actions may not reflect the love of Christ, which they talk about so earnestly.

Activists think they can force the kingdom of God to come by their own energy and ideas; they use politics and programs to try to save the world rather than depending upon the power of God.

In contrast, I said, the Transcendent position is the goal toward which all spiritual growth should move; to stop in any corner other than this was to miss the plan of God for every human life. I implied that the Traditionalist was too indifferent and self-satisfied, the Authoritarian too selfish and ego-centered, and the Activist too worldly and self-directed. God wants a relationship with us, I explained, and if we seek first the Transcendent position, then all the other qualities will be added to us and Christ will send us back into the other three areas with new authority and power. I planned to call the Transcendent corner the "T-Corner" for short and to use that term as the title of the book.

When I gave the outline to some responsible people whose views on the church I deeply respect, I started getting questions such as these: "What about the legitimate authority of Scripture?" "What about the great traditions and liturgies of the Church?" "What about Jesus' command to take the gospel actively into all the world?" "You have minimized three-quarters of what is going on in the church. Why is that?"

Why was that indeed! The more I thought about it, the more it became obvious that because I happened to be exploring the transcendent area of the faith at that moment, I concluded that it was the most important of the four. Again, I was seeing things only from my own perspective. In doing so, I had overlooked the views and contributions of a majority of the people, simply because they did not happen to see things as I did. I was trying to write a book against prejudice, and I was basing it on a prejudiced premise! I had done it again! "Wretched man that I am! Who will deliver me from this body of death?" (Romans 7:24, RSV). Who will deliver me from this mind of prejudice, this open heart that insists on reacting in closed ways?

Obviously, I had not thought the matter through clearly enough. It appeared that God had given me a good idea, but that my mind was too small to deal with it adequately. It became clear that the insights necessary to flesh out the rest of the book could only come from others. If we are all parts of the one body, then all of our insights are partial and no one viewpoint is large enough to see the whole picture.

As I sought the knowledge and experience of others, I began to see the theme in a much larger scope. There are four positions, to be sure, but the best one is not the one I happen to be embracing at the moment. They are all essential, both to the church and to an individual's faith. Those who hold, at a given moment, a different position from mine, far from being wrong, have something basic to give me that I can learn only from them.

It becomes clear upon investigation that there are at least three applications that can be made of this theme. The basic structure of the four positions and their interrelated value can be found in an individual's

personal faith, in his or her local church, and in the Christian church
as a whole. Let us look at these three areas and see how our model
helps us to understand them better.

Individual Faith

At one point in the development of this idea of the four positions, I
shared it with a group of ministers who were part of a study group in
which I was involved, and I asked for constructive criticism. One fellow
pastor, a younger man, asked a pertinent question: "Where do you see
yourself fitting into the picture?" It was an obvious question, but one
I have never faced directly. Perhaps I assumed that I was in the Transcendent position. I don't know. But in answering the question, I began
to see how the model we are using can be the profile of a person's
spiritual pilgrimage.

I answered the question by relating the story of my own struggle and
growth in faith. I began life in the Traditional position. My father's
father and brother were both ministers, and I was taken to church
regularly from my earliest days. I sat between my parents every Sunday
of my growing-up years, attended every level of Sunday school, sang
in the adult choir, and was president of the youth groups. My mother
was the youth advisor; my father was the Sunday school superintendent.
Together they were the first couple in that church's history who were
both ordained as ruling elders. The organist was my piano teacher, and
the minister was a family friend. There was no escape for me. The
church was a central element in our lives, and though we never talked
about "salvation" and "commitment," it was clear that there were
things one did and things one did not do because God was God.

Somewhere along the line, in my high school years, I began to
consider the ministry. It was about that time that I took the Authoritarian
position. If I was going to be a minister, I had to act as though I knew
what I was talking about. I joined study groups. I argued with my
biology teacher that the theory of evolution contradicted the Bible. I
went away to camp and was indoctrinated with the difference between
those who were saved and those who were lost forever. I joined little
prayer cells that prayed for the lost by name, and I felt a wonderful
sense of superiority and safety in the knowledge that since I was praying
for the lost, I must be saved. Even as a pastor of my first church, I
went to a local Nazarene minister's home and argued with him through
one entire afternoon, trying to convince him of the error of his ways,
certain that his fundamentalist theology was due to faulty thinking.

Gradually, as I was exposed to wiser people and to more diverse
ways of thinking, I became more tolerant and plunged into the next

phase of my spiritual development, the Activist approach. I was convinced that to be a successful minister meant to have a massive program raging in the church at every moment, something for everyone, so that people kept pouring into the building. It didn't really matter what they were doing just as long as something got them there. The really superior pastor was the one with enough imagination to design a program that would appeal to everyone. Being an activist also meant that I had to be everywhere, visible at all times, and constantly out in the world making contacts. As a result, I was secretary of this, treasurer of that, and a member of the boards of two or three agencies at a time; I served as trustee of an arts center and wrote articles for the newspaper. I did all of this while trying to run the church program almost single-handedly. It was my job to make the kingdom come, and I really tried!

In time, mercifully, I moved on. I do not know whether it was the intervention of the Spirit, the weariness from ''doing good,'' or the simple decrepitude of middle age, but gradually I discovered that it is also possible to serve God by sitting, reading, praying, or talking quietly to one person at a time about the meaning of spiritual growth. I began to seek the guidance of the Spirit in trying to find what God wanted me to do rather than forever telling God what I was prepared to do for the kingdom. I must now confess that I feel very much at home in the Transcendent position; and yet it is a temptation to sit all day and fly away into spiritual delights while the world burns down around me and people cry into ears that have stopped listening. In my single-minded pursuit of the truth (or was it simply intellectual narrow-mindedness?), I have always been willing to claim that the position I took at the moment was the best of all possible positions. But this journey of faith upon which I have been embarked for two generations has revealed to me the rich variety of experiences available to the Christian disciple, experiences that, I believe, can only be explored fully one at a time. To miss any one of them, to settle in a particular position and take root there is to deny what God has prepared for us—a depth experience that will not only make our own faith four-dimensional but will give us a firsthand understanding of those who take all the various positions.

The Local Church

If one can understand the personal spiritual pilgrimage that has just been described, then it is easy to conclude that any local congregation is a collection of people, each of whom is in the midst of a unique journey. Thus, in an average congregation, each of the four positions has its own contingent, and that distinctive distribution has tremendous significance in the life of that church. Among other things, it has an effect on whether there is peace or disharmony in the church family; it explains the presence of cliques; it determines whether the congregation will be considered conservative or liberal; it has a bearing on what kind of preaching the congregation wants to hear; and it exerts its influence on the outsider who is considering membership in the group.

In the typical church family there is a whole range of likes and dislikes, and on every issue some people can be counted upon for support and others for opposition. Normally, this circumstance is perceived in a general way, but the dynamics are not clearly understood since there are no guidelines upon which the leadership can base an analysis.

Using the four-position model, however, the issues of conflict and division begin to be seen as logical extensions of four clearly understood positions. Thus, the varieties of interaction and response to a given issue can be more readily predicted. Let us look at several examples.

We should note that for this purpose we have simplified the positions we are describing. Very few people fall into a single category—pure Authoritarian, for example. Usually a person is a unique mixture of all four, with a heavier emphasis on one position that determines how he or she will react in most cases. But in other instances, because of a strong element of, say, the Traditional, a person will respond in ways that seem to be unaccountable, or at least uncharacteristic of an Authoritarian. This mixing is to be expected since we have all been influenced by a number of elements in our makeup. For the purposes of the following discussion, however, we will talk as if people hold exclusively to one position or another.

Mutual Perception

One of the most unsettling discoveries for those who work in the church is that Christians do not always act in loving ways toward other Christians. This was also true of the early church, which frequently suffered from disagreement over doctrine and practice. Yet those first Christians were united by circumstances far different from those faced by most believers today. At that time they were bound tightly together by their common spiritual experience as well as by the world's rejection, and they discovered the intense unity that comes from mutual dependence.

Today it is different. Christians, at least in the free world, are no longer rejected by the world, and their primary associations are no longer limited to those within the community of faith. Because dependence upon other Christians is not essential to their survival, there is less intimacy among Christians, resulting in less understanding of varying points of view. Thus, while people still congregate with other

Christians, at least in their churches, they generally choose as intimates those who share their religious point of view. This creates distance between different theological groups within the church and tends to foster suspicion, mutual rejection, and sometimes hostility. People are likely to dramatize these feelings by using descriptive names for those in other groups. Such names reveal a great deal about the people using them and about their perception of those whom they are describing.

A chart of some of these characterizations is printed below. These are not the only names that might be used since the matter is highly subjective. But the following terms, all of which I have heard used in these connections, serve to illustrate the point. Those in the left-hand column often refer to those in the box by using the following terms:

	Traditionalist	Authoritarian	Activist	Transcendent
Traditionalist		fanatic	do-gooder	Holy-Roller
Authoritarian	scriptural illiterate		liberal	unbiblical
Activist	indifferent	reactionary		unrealistic
Transcendent	unconverted	legalist	worldly	

A Traditionalist may see an Authoritarian as a "fanatic," while the latter considers the careful study of Scripture and the desire to share it with others as the most obvious of Christian disciplines. In the reverse case, the Authoritarian, seeing the Traditionalist involved with building, finance, and program but not particularly interested in scriptural studies or the pursuit of a personal relationship with Christ, may condemn her for spending time on the externals of faith and brand her a "scriptural illiterate." "It is not the institution that saves us," the Authoritarian may insist. "It is the Word of God. How can you say you believe in God and not be constantly dependent upon God's Word?"

In another pairing, the Transcendent may look at the Authoritarian, who quotes the Scripture in detail, and call him a legalist, a head-tripper, or a new kind of Pharisee because of his emphasis on law. "Grace," says the Transcendent, "not law, is the basis of salvation." But the Authoritarian, often suspicious of feelings, will condemn the Transcendent for her amorphous faith, her emphasis on ecstatic feeling, her subjectivism. "We need to be objective," he says. "We need to base ourselves on God's truth, not our own feelings. Your lust for feeling good spiritually is unbiblical self-indulgence." "The Spirit leads us to grace," says the Transcendent. "The Bible leads us to truth," counters the Authoritarian. And they are both right. But coming at the matter from opposite directions, they each see only part of the truth, and, in trying to protect themselves from aspects of faith that they do not understand, they resort to name-calling.

Group Formation

One of the insights I gained from using this model to help me understand my own congregation had to do with the diverse groups that spring up in the church. The model helped me to see how the groups begin, who supports them, and where they do their work.

In general, Traditionalists tend to support groups that (1) are sponsored by some official agency of the denomination, (2) are organized in most local congregations within the denomination, and (3) are tied together by an area-wide, denominationally recognized body. For instance, one type of group that Traditionalist women support is the missionary circle. It has a long history in the local church and is supported by denominational materials. Similar groups exist in other congregations of the same denomination in the area, and the program is enriched by regional meetings. Men in the Traditionalist position are attracted to denominational men's associations, which tend to have the same support structure. If the groups combine with other churches, they generally seek out those within their own denomination. People with these preferences seem to be influenced by the institutional base on which the group is founded because it gives them a sense of being part of a larger permanent organization.

In contrast, the Transcendent, perhaps because she finds few institutionally organized groups in the mainline churches that support her quest for spiritual growth, will organize her own group in the local church. When she seeks a larger fellowship, she does not hesitate to go outside the denomination to groups that are ecumenical in structure. Her need to stay within the denomination is not as strong as that of the Traditionalist. Her spiritual needs bring her into contact with others who are also searching, and she meets with them regardless of heritage, sometimes totally outside the organized church.

The Authoritarian tends to remain within his own church but demands that the church keep faith with his own deepest beliefs. He gravitates toward Bible study groups that help him clarify his beliefs or groups that discuss the need to strengthen the denomination's work or correct its wrongs. For this purpose, the Authoritarian will seek out those in other churches of the same denomination who think as he does; together they will, if they feel it necessary, form their own grass-roots organization, which may function on the fringes of the denomination, seeing itself in a watchdog role. While the Traditionalist works within denominationally sponsored programs, the Authoritarian may at times find himself in opposition to the denomination and may even threaten secession if it does not adhere to the truth as he sees it. This may be because the Traditionalist perceives the institution as permanent and superior, while the Authoriatarian sees truth as superior, feeling that the institution must be answerable to the individual and to the local church.

The Activist uses the church as a base but feels that society itself should be the focus of her work. As a result, her groups will center on social needs—hunger, delinquency, justice—and she will align with those from other churches and from the community at large who share the same goals. She crosses the denominational barrier to accomplish her ministry, as does the Transcendent, but whereas the latter tends to remain in a church context to conduct her group work, the Activist focuses her action on the community itself, because it is there she sees the need to exist.

In other words, the Traditionalist and the Authoritarian both tend to work with members of their own denomination, the former primarily interested in programs wholly contained within the denomination's structure and the latter occasionally working outside the denomination. Even in these cases, however, the Authoritarian usually does not work closely with those of other denominations, since the focus of his work is the improvement of conditions within his own church organization.

In contrast, the Transcendent and the Activist both seek others from the community who share their interest, the former usually retaining some form of church orientation, the latter focusing on the community itself.

These different types of groups cover the whole range of work and experience that is open to the Christian. The Traditionalist works within the denomination, but the Authoritarian does not allow the denomination to dominate him. The Transcendent is at home with other Christians in their churches, and the Activist works with those of different backgrounds to help the community become the kingdom. None of these groups, alone, is able to do everything, but through the associations into which people divide themselves because of their varied interests, all aspects of the work are accomplished. "There are many parts, but one body" (1 Corinthians 12:20). It looks almost as though God planned it that way!

Individual Preferences

If individuals occupy one of the four positions, so do congregations. Many churches have a dominant viewpoint, and it is important that the pastor quickly discover which one it is.

In order to get congregational input for my preaching, I have through the years sent around questionnaires asking the people what they wanted me to preach about. Some of the responses were predictable: prayer, salvation, suffering. The most specific suggestions were of questionable value: "How can my husband get a job?" "Why do you neglect preaching on the genealogies?" But anyone who has gone through this effort realizes that the responses fall roughly into four categories, which come directly from the four different positions.

Traditionalists want to hear preaching on such questions as: "Who is God?" "How does my faith fit into my daily work?" "What do the Old Testament stories have to say to me today?" "What do I need to learn from the creeds and confessions of the church?" Sermons on conversion, sanctification, and witnessing often cause discomfort to those in this position.

Authoritarians want to hear Bible preaching. If the person in the pulpit gets too socially oriented or preaches topical sermons for too many Sundays, he or she will probably hear from the Authoritarians in the flock. "Pastor, I come to hear the Word. I want to take something home that will make the Bible come alive for me." Often those holding this position will respond positively when a sermon on sin and its consequences is preached and may actually say something like, "It's all right to talk about the love of God, but we can't forget the wrath of God!" It is almost as though they need to hear a little hellfire from time to time, as though the voice from the pulpit speaking about the justice of God provides them with the necessary stimulus to keep them on the straight path.

Those in the Activist position include people who carry a burden for a variety of causes, some popular, some on the liberal fringe of the congregation's interest. A preacher is expected to speak about mission and to urge people to demonstrate "the grace of liberality." But in some congregations, preaching about the poor and hungry, even those in the local areas, sparks disagreement. The Traditionalists and especially the Authoritarians may respond, "If they want to eat, let them work!" Activists involved in particular projects will want to hear support from the pulpit for their work and may expect to hear sermons on race relations, sexism, school integration, and a number of other such topics. Many of these issues are important to the so-called "liberals," and Activists, more than those in the other three positions, see a close relationship between religion and politics. Interestingly, Authoritarians also may suggest that the preacher address political topics, but these topics tend to be on the opposite end of the spectrum from those of the Activist—the need for a strong national defense, the obligation to support Israel, the reinstatement of prayer in the public schools. The preacher who deals with politics of any stripe had better know which position the people are in if he or she wants to avoid being surprised by their response.

The Transcendents are likely to ask for sermons on prayer, on sanctification, on spiritual growth, and related topics. They tend to be bored with intellectual presentations or those that deal with church history and theology. This does not mean that Transcendents are not intelligent or that they are uninterested in history and theology. But what they want in preaching is inspiration, a pure vision of the transcendent God, a time of fellowship with a personal Jesus. I have often had someone come to me from this group and say, "That was a head trip you took us on today. I *know* what you think. What I want to know is whether you believe it!" The preaching that is most effective for those in this position is celebration, a verbal encounter from heart to heart that lets the people in the pews know that the person in the pulpit has had the same experience. They need to sense the preacher's integrity, his or her freedom to speak about personal experience, some evidence that his or her faith comes from an encounter with a living God and not just from a seminary course. These people talk about being "fed" by the sermon and will indicate sooner than the others that the fare served them has been thin and unnourishing.

How does all this change the way a person preaches? Perhaps not at all. Preachers have their own integrity to maintain; they are answerable to God and not to the majority of the congregation. But if they are not aware of the dynamics in their congregations, they may be inviting years of suffering for themselves and the people of the church. If an Activist stands in the pulpit of a church primarily composed of Authoritarians, not only may she feel as though she is speaking to the wind, not only may she sense hostility from some of the people, but over the years her work may actually have the result of hardening their attitudes against the very position she is trying to establish. A Transcendent in the pulpit of a Traditional church, especially one who is a charismatic, may have a divisive effect on the congregation because of the temptation to cluster with the few who are more vocal about their faith and who speak the same spiritual language. In the process, others may get the sense that they are on the outside, that their faith is somehow inferior.

Certain safeguards seem to be built into the system, however. For instance, an Activist church seldom calls a Traditional minister, in the same way that a Transcendent church shies away from calling an Authoritarian to its pulpit. There are different kinds of preachers just as there are different emphases in the churches, and a sense of creating a proper match guides both parties in making their decisions. Sometimes this is clearly understood, but often it is simply a sense that "we feel comfortable together." I am certain that the Holy Spirit works in the majority of cases to see that there is a good marriage. In those cases where the alliance is not marked by happiness and "divorce" seems to be threatening, it can often be traced to the fact that the minister is holding one position and the majority of his or her people are in another, and neither of them is willing to move.

Christian love, of course, can overcome even the most peculiar mismatches. Spiritual growth comes about when pastors and congregations have views somewhat different from each other's. I have observed, over the two decades I have spent in this church, that the half-dozen larger Protestant churches in our town have frequently called pastors who are somewhat more liberal than the congregation itself. There seems to be a subconscious knowledge, an undefined wisdom, that tells them that calling a minister who thinks exactly as they do is asking for stagnation. Unless there is some creative tension in a congregation, there will be no impulse to move, to grow, to broaden their understanding of the gospel's implications. Preachers ought to be seen as agents of change. If they are not apart from the people in some direction—more spiritual, more mission oriented, more focused on Scripture—what do they have to teach the people of the church? In what direction will they call the people to move? Therefore, what we are looking for is not a perfect match. The knowledge of the four positions can be used to prevent a disastrous mismatch, but the right ideal might be to seek purposely some creative tension in establishing a new pastoral relationship. One of our local congregations—old, established, traditional, and located in the heart of the decaying center of the city—recently called an Activist minister specifically so that he could help them develop an activist ministry to the needy people in their area. The relationship will cause pain, surely, because it will mean learning a whole new set of answers to the question "What is the church?" But the people are doing this with their eyes open, and I believe that because they know what they are doing, they will succeed.

It is not the mismatches that produce disharmony and separation. All four positions need to be represented in every congregation and heard from every pulpit. What produces crisis is when one side or the other moves too fast or refuses to move at all. We are in the church to learn and to grow; if we refuse to grow, not even the apostle Paul could lead us into the kingdom.

The Larger Church

What we have said in this chapter is also true with regard to the different churches within a community and to the various denominations in the worldwide Christian church.

For instance, if a mainline church and a charismatic church exist side by side on Main Street, each may have the strong conviction that its own message is holding up a pure witness for the community while the church next door is working in ignorance of the truth. But the fact is that, in a larger sense, each of them is filling a role that ensures that the gospel *in its fullness* is preached in that community. The mainline church may be providing a Traditional ministry (though it is certainly not limited to this; its role may be any of the other three), while the charismatic church may be ministering to those in the Transcendent position. The church across town perhaps will have an emphasis on a position that is neglected by these two, and a fourth church somewhere in the vicinity may fill the final position so that, according to some divine impulse, all aspects of the Good News are offered to the residents of that area. We can see this as part of the plan of God, but that plan doubtless works itself out through the people from all four positions who live in that community and seek the fellowship of others who think as they do. Thus they divide themselves into congregations in which they express the one truth through different emphases. In the design of God, they are all working together. The irony is that they seldom see that design.

Paul deals with this in the fourth chapter of Ephesians. In the eleventh and twelfth verses he says,

> It was [Christ] who "gave gifts to mankind"; he appointed some to be apostles, others to be prophets, others to be evangelists, others to be pastors and teachers. He did this to prepare all God's people for the work of Christian service, in order to build up the body of Christ.

It takes little imagination to see in this description the completeness of the four positions we have been describing. Paul says that Christ did not intend for everyone to do everything but that he *appointed* some to do certain tasks and others to perform different duties. However, the purpose of his appointing them to do their various tasks was "in order to build up the body of Christ."

What are the offices he lists? *Apostles:* could these have been the first Christian Traditionalists, the ones who lived with Christ, who represent the whole church and its historical continuity? *Prophets:* perhaps these are Transcendents who live in the presence of God, who hear God's Word in its purity and who lift us up so that we can hear it also. *Evangelists:* these are certainly Activists, whose duty it is to go out and make disciples, to take the Good News to those who would otherwise never hear it. *Pastors and Teachers:* these might be the Authoritarians, who through their own study and spiritual experience guide others along the way of true belief and practice.

You may find other ways of applying these designations; the roles all overlap to some extent. But the fact is that Christ did not appoint an apostle to be an evangelist or a teacher to be a prophet. Certainly an apostle has teaching duties and an evangelist must prophesy, but Paul says, ''He appointed *some* to be apostles, *others* to be evangelists,'' and so on. In the same way, can we not say that he appointed some to be Authoritarians, others to be Transcendents, others to be Activists, and still others to be Traditionalists? By his appointment all the tasks are accomplished, although no one does everything, and the body of Christ is built up. We all have a specialty, and we need to see it as a part of the whole ministry of the church. We need to avoid, on the one hand, looking upon that individual task as the whole gospel and, on the other hand, thinking that we have to be specialists in all four positions at the same time.

Paul has an interesting phrase in Ephesians 4:3. He says, ''*Do your best* to preserve the unity which the Spirit gives. . . .'' How sensitive to the failings of human nature that statement is! We will never be able to do it perfectly, but our goal must be to ''grow up in every way to Christ,'' to ''reach to the very height of Christ's full stature,'' to find our place as a cell or as an organ in the infinite spiritual organism that is the kingdom. We must strive to fit our incompleteness into Christ's perfection, so that ''under his control all the different parts of the body fit together. . . . When each separate part works as it should, the whole body grows and builds itself up through love'' (Ephesians 4:13-16).

7

The Unity That
the Spirit Gives

According to the Gospel of Mark a teacher of the Law asked Jesus, "Which commandment is the most important of all?" Jesus, in answering, recited the Shema from Deuteronomy 6:4: "Hear, O Israel: The Lord our God, the Lord is one." Then he continued on into the next verse, which reads in Deuteronomy 6:5, "And you shall love the Lord your God with all your heart, and with all your soul, and with all your might." When Jesus recited this verse, however, he added a phrase: "And you shall love the Lord your God with all your heart, and with all your soul, *and with all your mind*, and with all your strength" (Mark 12:29-30, emphasis added).

The addition of that fourth idea, loving God with our minds, apparently filled in for Jesus an element that was missing in the original Old Testament statement. It also makes it possible, conveniently, for us to fit his answer neatly into the design we have been developing. When Jesus talked about "heart," "soul," "mind," and "strength," it seems apparent he was referring to the four areas we are discussing. He said that the greatest commandment is to love God with our heart (caring for others—Activist), with our soul (seeking spiritual fellowship with God—Transcendent), with our mind (studying and learning his truth—Authoritarian), and with our strength (building and maintaining the institution—Traditionalist). If Jesus believed that these ideas represent completeness in our service to God, perhaps his statement can assure us that our four-position approach to discipleship includes the elements about which Jesus was most concerned.

Let us consider at this point that our human growth consists of both an active stage and a reflective stage. At first we are motivated by the biological needs of self-preservation (food and shelter) and continuing the species (including sexual expression, nest building, and child rearing). Later in life we draw back from the active phase to assimilate

and integrate what we have experienced, to "gain wisdom." The midlife
crisis comes at the point when we realize that we have had "all our
eggs in one basket" for too long, when we begin to regret that we have
been neglecting other important areas of our lives. At that point, we
consciously attempt to achieve a new overall balance. This is probably
accompanied by some degree of transfer in the hemispheric dominance
in our brains; if we have been left-side dominant all of our lives—
physical, structured, intellectual—we may make a conscious effort to
balance that dominance by learning right-side skills, by becoming more
artistic, more sympathetic, and person-oriented rather than thing-ori-
ented. This is a way of balancing the male-female elements in ourselves
so that we become as complete and rounded as possible. It is a process
through which we come to terms with a dimension of ourselves to
which we previously had been blind, a self-discovery that changes us
from two-dimensional to three-dimensional. This process helps us to
see the larger implications of life and to appreciate the differences in
others.

The same process occurs in spiritual growth. We all enter the family
of faith at some point. If our parents bring us into the church in our
youth, it may be by way of the Traditional position. If we are converted
through a college Bible fellowship, we may begin at the Authoritarian
or the Transcendent position. If we grow up in a needy area where the
world seems hostile and people turn to the church for leadership and
hope, perhaps we will come into the church by way of the Activist
position. Wherever we begin, we tend to explore that position fully
until we are bored with that experience and sense a need for something
more or until some event pushes us into a new area of discovery. This
exploration of the different positions may continue, one at a time, until
we have occupied each position for a while. Each time we move, we
have more information, a broader background, and our attitude toward
each new position is modified by our knowledge of the others we have
experienced. Finally, we can integrate the values of all four positions
and move to a new perspective, where we are no longer emotionally
invested in any one position. Our goal at that point is to become what
Jesus desires every follower to be, a person who loves God with his
or her whole being, not with just part of it.

As I have said, my spiritual growth involved a series of individual
experiences in each position, one at a time. I entered the Traditionalist
position with my parents, moved to the Authoritarian position because
of the influence of friends, occupied the Activist position for a time

because of my conviction that this was the duty of a pastor, and finally discovered the Transcendent position, through a sense of need or weariness or the grace of God—or all three. But each succeeding position was set in a larger context. When I was a Traditionalist, the other three positions were either invisible or seemed foolish to me. When I became an Authoritarian, I could understand those who worked through the institutional church but not those who sponsored nonchurch ministries or who were highly vocal about their personal religious experiences. While I was an Activist, most of the other styles of behavior in the church made sense to me, but I still felt uncomfortable around, and therefore considered myself superior to, Transcendents. Finally, even that ignorance was overcome. I felt a passionate involvement in each area as I experienced it, but the quality of that feeling changed as I moved through the positions. At first I felt the passion that arises from ignorance, from not understanding the other areas and therefore being convinced that I was right and they were wrong. Later, along with fuller understanding, came the passionate joy of knowing that the system of differences in the church all fits together and makes sense, that God is indeed in charge, and that I can leave the church in God's hands without having to tell God how to run it.

When a person arrives at this point, he or she is excited to be able to function in any of the four positions at a given moment or in all the positions at once, to be able to come and go as the need requires, so that he or she might help to lead someone to Christ from any one of the perspectives. How can I identify with a person unless I have held his or her position for a time? The active phase of spiritual growth— moving through the positions—helps us to learn about the whole range of work that needs to be done in the kingdom. When we master that knowledge, we can be useful to all of God's people, regardless of which quarter they come from.

How does this all work out in real life? If our theory is correct, then every person we meet is somewhere in the process of movement among the four positions. That knowledge can affect how we deal with others. Let us take a fairly common example of how this works in two different lives.

Two people start out in the Traditionalist position. Their parents take them, as children, to the same church, before they learn that there are some people who don't go to church every Sunday morning. The two friends are active together in the church's program as they grow up and understand church to be an essential part of their lives. Then they graduate from high school. One goes to college; the other enters a local business. The college student finds a church near campus that employs a youth minister to work with the college students. The minister is an Activist, convinced that the church has an obligation to the world to take purposeful steps to hasten the coming of the kingdom. The minister is full of enthusiasm, involved in specific projects, and is able to arouse the idealism of the students. Under this leadership, our young student becomes part of a group that sponsors an Activist ministry, supporting liberal causes in the university town, enlisting the intellectuals on campus to support what they are doing, and obeying Christ's commission to respond to the world's needs in his name.

Meanwhile, the young businesswoman gets married and assumes leadership in the church of her youth. She is concerned about her community, about creating a climate in which she can safely rear her children—a climate of law and order, of decency and morality. She sees this as a continuation of her early training in the church, and joins a study group to deepen her understanding of Christian citizenship. The result of her group experience is a sense of frustration that so few people see a connection between the breakdown of morality in society and the growing indifference toward religion. The group begins to campaign for a return to faith, for a restatement of the fundamental truths of the gospel, and for the suppression of those modern ideas that threaten to destabilize the old traditions.

The two friends meet several years later and discover that although they once held the same ideas about God and the church, they are now worlds apart. Each looks at the other in astonishment and asks, ''What happened to you? How can you think like that? How did you ever get so far away from the truth?'' Gradually, almost unknowingly, one has drifted into an area we would call ''liberal'' while the other has developed attitudes that are referred to as ''conservative.'' Starting from the same point, they have moved in opposite directions; the businesswoman has moved to the Authoritarian position; the college student has crossed over into the Activist area. Without realizing it, they have assumed positions within the four-position structure that have the greatest perceived differences between them. As liberals and conservatives sometimes see each other as adversaries, so Authoritarians and Activists often think that those in the other position misunderstand the gospel or that they are doing just the opposite of what the gospel requires.

Suppose our two friends continue to pursue their own spiritual growth for another ten years. The businesswoman eventually becomes tired of the sterility of the thinking in her group, while the college graduate is less and less enchanted with the results of his activist efforts. They both sense the need for some inner growth that goes beyond the ideas they have been promoting for so long. In search of a more personal sense of the reality of God, they both happen to join the same spiritual-growth group in another church in the community. Once again, they find themselves sitting alongside each other. They are surprised to discover that they are both saying the same things, that they are both spiritually restless, that their old ideas are no longer adequate. While they still believe those ideas, they need something more. They begin to pray together with members of the group. They discover meditation and begin to share some of the mystical things that are happening to them. They find in their sharing a deeper, more joyful sense of the goodness and purpose of God than they have ever known before. They bring to their discussion, however, totally different stories. Together now in the Transcendent position, they learn from each other. They each gain an understanding of the other's former position, the one they have not as yet explored. They achieve in their new relationship a vision of the fullness of the kingdom that previously had been hidden from them.

If we see the Authoritarian-Activist split representing the division between conservatives and liberals, we can call the division between Transcendents and Traditionalists the ''Mary-Martha split.'' We will speak more about this later. The gulf between Traditionalists and Transcendents also illustrates the tension between division and unity. In the Traditionalist position, the emphasis on one's own church and denomination, on one's own way of doing things, can be divisive. In the Transcendent position, the emphasis on Christ can be inclusive, counteracting the estrangement created by denominationalism. As we talk about ourselves and our churches, we tend to draw apart from those in other churches and emphasize our differences. As we talk about Christ and his claim on us, we find a unity that transcends denomination and we focus on our similarities. The tension in the Traditionalist-Transcendent split is between what we owe to the body of Christ and what we owe to the kingdom of God, or how we divide our obligations to the visible and the invisible church. The Traditionalist position teaches us the value of the local; the Transcendent, the value of the universal.

When Jesus told us that we need to love God with heart, soul, mind, and strength, he was referring to a number of dimensions of existence in which we need to achieve wholeness. Let us look at some of these.

Focus

Each of the four positions has a different focus. We can graph these differences as follows:

Traditionalists focus on history; they look backward at what has been done, at "the way we've always done it." The focus of Authoritarians is on themselves and their understanding of the eternal truth of God. Therefore, their vision turns inward toward the ideas through which they maintain a relationship with God. Activists, on the other hand, focus outside themselves on others who have a special need for the love and compassion of Christ. And Transcendents, striving for a relationship with the Eternal, keep their focus on God. In all four groups we find the lordship and the guidance of Christ: in history as we read of his ministry and resurrection; within ourselves as we sense God's sovereignty over us; in others as we serve by caring for the least of Christ's brothers and sisters; and in God as we meet God in the timeless Word, the creative principle behind all of life. The focus of our work is not one-dimensional, and Christ is not to be found only in one place. As we combine all of these foci, we find them producing a multidimensional discipleship, the unity that the Spirit gives.

1 Corinthians 13

The passage on love in 1 Corinthians 13 also shows us how the four positions cover the whole range of life within the kingdom. Paul introduces these verses by speaking of the "lesser" gifts (in chapter twelve), concluding with the words "Best of all, however, is the following way," by which he means love. As he begins the chapter on love, he reiterates the former gifts, saying that, while they are important, they accomplish nothing if they are not backed by love. The chapter ends with the well-known thirteenth verse: "These three remain: faith, hope, and love; and the greatest of these is love."

If we display in the following arrangement the gifts of which Paul speaks, we see that they cover all the elements we have described.

73632

a. The "lesser" gifts are certainly those of the institutional church—languages of men, inspired preaching, knowledge, sacrifice—and describe the Traditionalist corner. These gifts are essential to the church, but by themselves they are incomplete.

b. Faith, one of the three final qualities mentioned by Paul, refers to the work of the Authoritarian corner. A dictionary definition for faith is "the assent of the mind to the truth of what God has revealed." Faith involves the knowledge of things unseen, the disciplining of our mental skills to express the truth of God. But without love, the product of those skills becomes sterile and cold.

c. Hope, the second of the remaining qualities, fits the Transcendent corner because it describes our trust in the goodness and wisdom of God. Faith believes what it cannot prove; hope follows when it cannot see where it is being led, trusting that the destination will be cause for joy and thanksgiving. Without love, hope becomes a selfish search for private salvation.

d. Love, "the greatest of these," describes the work of the Activist corner. Jesus makes it clear that love is the central requirement—specifically, love directed toward others: "Now I give you a new commandment: love one another. As I have loved you, so you must love one another. If you have love for another, then everyone will know that you are my disciples" (John 13:34-35). Notice that love is not referred to as the only gift. Even though Paul calls it the greatest gift, the rest are still essential; without them, there would be no framework through which love could work.

Jung's Types

One of the lasting legacies of the Swiss psychiatrist Carl Jung is his description of psychological types. He believed that all conscious mental activity fell into four categories: sensing and intuition (two differing ways of perceiving reality) and thinking and feeling (two ways in which judgments are made). Jung said of his theory:

I have been asked almost reproachfully why I speak of four functions and not of more or fewer. That there are exactly four is a matter of empirical fact. . . . A certain completeness is attained by these four. Sensation establishes what is actually given, thinking enables us to recognize its meaning, feeling tells us its value, and finally intuition points to the possibilities of the whence and whither that lie within the immediate facts. . . . The four functions are somewhat like the four points of the compass; they are just as arbitrary and just as indispensable.[1]

The Myers-Briggs Type Indicator provides us with an instrument to differentiate among the varying types. A number of authors, among them David Keirsey and Gordon Lawrence, have expanded upon the concept, describing in detail the personality characteristics of the four types, their strengths and weaknesses.[2]

This body of information has made us aware that we should learn to value the strengths in others rather than assuming that, since they function differently than we do, they are of necessity "wrong." Since that idea is also the thesis of this book, let us see if the several functions identified by Jung correspond to the variations within the model we have been discussing.

The four types in Jung's system compose two sets of opposing or complementary traits. The first set describes the tension between sensing and intuiting, caused by using the physical senses to deal with the external world on the one hand, and using the inner senses to perceive the internal world of the spirit on the other. In our model, this same tension exists in the two "T" corners and expresses the differences between Traditionalists and Transcendents.

Sensing people are described as realistic, aware of the present, interested in the value of experience and therefore concerned with how things were done in the past. This focus on the present produces a desire to know how a thing is relevant in practical use, leading to an interest in facts and detail. Sensing persons are most comfortable doing things systematically and in a conventional way; they are routine-oriented, earthbound, focused on the concrete. This is a description of the person we have identified as a Traditionalist, one who is interested in the outer realities of religion. Traditionalists concentrate on the minutiae of running the institution; they want what is done today to build logically upon the past. Traditionalists measure the success of any program by its practical effect upon such things as membership growth and financial contributions; they focus on external expressions of the faith—buildings, traditions, procedures—and expect to have things done in a familiar way. They do not spend as much time theorizing about the future of religion as they do dealing with the concrete needs of the church today.

Intuitive people are just the opposite. While Sensibles (Sensing people) are described as realistic, Intuitives are comfortable with abstract
and symbolic relationships. Sensibles are invested in the present; Intuitives look to the future, certain that anything that exists can be
improved. They rely on inspiration and insight rather than experience,
concentrating on future possibilities. While Sensing people look for the
practical, Intuitives reach for the possible, the theoretical, what might
be rather than what is. In place of facts, Intuitives live with metaphor,
imagery, dreams, and poetry, forsaking convention for creative imagining. They are innovative, other worldly and speculative. This is clearly
a profile of the persons this book identifies as Transcendents. Abstract
rather than concrete, Transcendents tend to deal with the inner spiritual
realities of religion—prayer, meditation, visions—rather than with its
outer trappings; they are more interested in the abstract kingdom of
God than the stone church building down the block. Sensible/Tradi-
tionalists concern themselves with the physical setting and continuity
of religion. Intuitive/Transcendents are more interested in what goes
on in the building after it is built; therefore, they invest their energy in
creative expression: fantasy, song, story, and inspirational experiences
that uplift the spirit. Innovative and focused on the future, they are
bored by routine; they enjoy groups in which personal experience can
be shared and new truth discovered. While some people may look upon
them as impractical, they find more interest in the mystical relationship
with God than in concerning themselves with mundane details.

The second set of opposing functions in Jung's system is made up
of thinking and feeling. These two qualities point to the difference
between using logic or emotion to deal with the world; they reflect whether
it is more important to be impersonal or personal in making judgments.
In our model, this tension is between the two "A" corners, highlighting
the differences between Authoritarians and Activists.

The type Jung refers to as Thinking is characterized by impersonal
analysis, objectivity, impartiality, and a sense of fairness and justice.
Those of this type are logical, analytical, tough-minded people who
rely on principles, policies, and laws and who attempt to use logic to
decide conflicts. Authoritarians could be described in the same way. They
concern themselves with ideas rather than people, with objective truth
and precise ideas about how God's demands should control human
endeavor. Authoritarians think in a somewhat impersonal way because
this is how they see God dealing with the world, righteously enforcing

laws upon all people with no exceptions. The justice of this view
impresses them with the utter fairness of God, since all people are
equally accountable. Because Authoritarians see God's law as stable
and logical, their theological formulations are clear and well-organized,
emphasizing the fact that certain consequences follow inevitably from
basic principles.

The fourth, or Feeling, type is described as compassionate rather
than logical, empathetic rather than impersonal, and subjective rather
than objective. Instead of being rigidly impartial, Feeling people are
aware of extenuating circumstances and see the need to modify fairness
and justice with mercy and humaneness. Logical analysis is not as
important to them as harmony and peace, and they will go out of their
way to achieve understanding. They are sympathetic, while those at
the other end of the scale tend to be tough-minded. They find human
values more compelling than principles and laws. While Thinkers try
to win through logic, Feeling people attempt to prevail through persuasion. These qualities also describe the Activist, who puts people
above philosophies and who believes that as Christians we are specifically directed to help the last and the lost. Activists see Jesus in the
needy person, and feel that, since God showed love for us so dramatically in Christ, we should share that love with others in tangible ways.
Because they feel that love is more important than law, Activists will
offer help even when others may think it is inadvisable. They believe
that a kingdom based on law does not create harmony and peace nearly
as effectively as one based on love. Their final argument is that Jesus
said, "Whenever you did this for one of the least important of these
brothers of mine, you did it for me!" (Matthew 25:40).

A diagram of the four positions combined with the Jungian types
looks like this:

(Authoritarian)	(Transcendent)
Thinking	Intuiting
Sensing	Feeling
(Traditionalist)	(Activist)

One reason that Traditionalists and Transcendents find it so hard to
understand each other is that they often belong at opposite ends of the
Sensing-Intuiting continuum that Keirsey says causes more misunderstanding and separates people by a wider margin than any of the other
functional differences.[3] In our model we call this difference the Mary-

Martha split. The high level of misunderstanding arises because the two types choose fundamentally different styles within the church; one focuses on the visible church in the world, the other on the invisible church shrouded in the mystical.

There are also many possibilities for misunderstanding between the Thinking and Feeling types (Au/Ac). This, as we have said, is the Conservative-Liberal split and involves the debate over whether our first concern should be the ideas that come from God (theory) or the application of those ideas in a less-than-perfect world (practice). This debate raises fundamental questions: Do we function on an impartial or a personal basis? Do we focus on the overall plan or the individual need? Do we concern ourselves with theological or human values? Do we make law or grace our priority?

Modes of Awareness

It is possible to respond to our environment in at least four different modes, which might be displayed as follows:

thinking	being
existing	doing

What is the relevance of these modes for our four positions? The Traditionalist attitude, by itself, is directed toward the past and the present. It is bounded by Law and the Physical, and therefore is least influenced by the grace of God or the transcendent dimension of life. Thus, it is an elementary level of consciousness, the entrance point through which the individual can be introduced to the larger realities. Sometimes, like an infant, we go through the motions of life without being aware of why we have been given life. Buried in the physical, aware only of the routines of life, we have no reflective element in our consciousness at this point, only an awareness of what is and what has been. This elementary level of consciousness is what Paul speaks of in 1 Corinthians 13: "When I was a child, my speech, feelings, and thinking were all those of a child." In this state a person is simply existing; he or she is dormant, living life on the level of mere functioning, doing what has always been done and unenlightened by what might yet be. This is not to say that all Traditionalists function on this level; certainly this is far from true. Yet, there are many people in the

church who are not spiritually awake, who listen to a sermon without
the slightest flicker of recognition of the truth, who sing the hymns
without praise in their hearts, who listen to the prayers with no sense
that God could be near enough to touch them. Whether their numbers
are large or small, they exist. We need to recognize that this is the
basic life form from which God can create a disciple on fire with the
Spirit.

In the Authoritarian position, we exercise our thinking skills, and
we know we exist as children of God because we can think about God,
we can ponder God's laws, and we can make the intellectual decision
to follow and obey. Someone has said that Muslims, on entering a
mosque, remove their shoes and leave them outside, whereas Christians,
all too often, on entering a church, remove their brains and leave them
outside.[4] We were created with minds; we cannot love God with our
whole being unless somehow our minds are put to use in the service
of faith. One of the mind's chief uses is to doubt. Doubt is not the
opposite of faith; sin is the opposite of faith. Doubt forces us to work
through ideas that keep us from God so that intellectually, as well as
in every other way, we are captured by God. If our faith is not intellectually tenable, it is false. Science continues to discover new information that corresponds with what the Bible has always taught, thus
strengthening the intellectual foundation of our belief. If God is in fact
the Creator, then God is at the end of every avenue of investigation.
Our problem is not that we fail to use our minds but that we stop
thinking before reaching the conclusions that God wants us to discover.
Our brain is another means through which we can be led home to God;
when we do not use it for God, we are stealing one of God's possessions.

Activists engage in "doing," because they know that reflecting on
truth does no good unless we translate that truth into action. We can
claim to love God, but John asked us how we think we can love the
One whom we have not seen if we do not love the ones we see every
day. The great commandment comes in two dimensions—we must love
God and love our neighbor. Ideas about God that do not become positive
action for people are make-believe. God wants us to be up and doing.
Jesus told us in John 9:4, "As long as it is day, we must do the work
of him who sent me; night is coming when no one can work."

The fourth mode of awareness is "being," the quality that charac-
terizes the Transcendent. Perhaps this is the mode most difficult to
discover, the one of which we are most frightened. To some people
"being" seems to mean doing nothing, but that is a misperception.

"Existing" is empty stillness; "being" is stillness full of the presence and power of God. Those who are afraid of this mode of awareness are those who connect value with "doing"—"I am important only if I produce something that is important." This is the Mary-Martha tension mentioned earlier. The story in Luke 10 describes the two women in dramatically different terms: Mary, "who sat down at the feet of the Lord and listened to his teaching," and Martha, who "was upset over all the work she had to do." Martha's conviction that her productivity created her value was wrong. Certainly, it is important to produce, but it is a mistake to assume that it is the producing that makes God see us as worthwhile. What about those who are unable to produce? What about those who produce and yet do not learn or grow in the process? We need to see that any creation of God is inherently valuable. You and I have worth simply because we are, because God saw fit to create us. God looked at this handiwork—you and me—and called it good. So, "being" is nothing less than celebrating our creation in the presence of God, staying near God, reflecting on our life, laughing with God over the funny things that happen to us on our way to spiritual maturity, and recognizing that the value of our life will not be stamped on our record at the end of our days as the result of what we have done, but that it was stamped on our soul at the beginning of our life as the result of what Christ has done.

Understanding this takes a tremendous burden from our soul. This is, in fact, one of the chief gifts of the cross, the knowledge that we no longer have to prove our worth, that our value was given to us at the moment God thought us worth saving. So our freedom is twofold: we are set free from sin, which everyone recognizes; and we are also set free from the effort of daily having to prove our worth to God, which many people do not recognize. Because of this, the focus of each day is totally changed; we do not have to live in fear that we might not do enough to please God. Instead, we are free to discover the surprises that God has hidden for us in each day, surprises that provide growth for us as we find ways in which to help others.

I was working on this chapter one day and had planned to write all morning in order to get a certain section completed. I was in the middle of a flow of ideas when my secretary buzzed to say that a man was in her office who wanted to see me. He was a former member of the congregation who had moved to California some years ago. I had not seen him in several years and could not very well avoid the meeting, although it was not scheduled. As we visited, I kept struggling to keep certain ideas for the book in mind so that I would not forget them before he left. Strange thoughts floated through my head: *Wouldn't I be accomplishing more, Lord, if I were writing now rather than talking to this single individual? Why did you send him, Lord? If you want me to give him my attention, Lord, help me stop thinking about the book.*

Suddenly it became clear to me that the man wanted to talk about his spiritual growth, his emerging sense of the presence of God, his need for deeper trust. The conversation turned intimate and personal, and I started sharing things from my own life to help him understand that I had been through the same dark valley. It was a time of intense spiritual fellowship, a distinct and identifiable joy for me. At the end of our sharing he said, "No minister I have ever talked to has gotten down to the nitty-gritty with me like you just did." We prayed together, and as he left he confessed that this was the first time he had ever shared his faith with another person. And then he was gone.

I reflected for a long time on that experience. In the world's terms, we had been wasting time, sitting around chatting, talking about intangibles, squandering an hour and a half of precious morning work time. Surely, if the book was worth anything, it would have been more "productive" for me to have been working on it during that time, since many people would have been reached instead of just one. But God does not see it this way. During that time, we were "being," accepting what God had made us, realizing what we were—two needy souls reaching out for each other in love and touching God in the space between us. The book was on *my* schedule that morning. The meeting was on *God's* schedule for me. How sad it would have been at the last day to see a line through that appointment in the heavenly book, with a notation saying, "John couldn't keep this date this morning. He was busy being productive."

The Place of Christ in Our Model

Some who have looked through this manuscript have said that there seems to be no specific place for Christ in our model. "What do you do with him?" they ask. "All we see is people doing their own thing. How can they do it without Jesus Christ?"

Let me say this as a final word, before we get to more practical matters. The presence of Christ must be seen in every aspect of the four-cornered model we have been discussing, because he is there. In our tradition, we look back and see his life, death, and resurrection. In the authority that guides us, we hear him speaking: "I am the way, the truth, and the life. No one comes to the Father but by me." "You must be born again." In our activities, we reach out to touch others because he said that, next to loving God, there is nothing more important than loving others in his name. In our transcendent moments, we sit in Christ's presence, we feel his strength, we receive his direction, we deepen our will to obey. He is in every corner. He must be, or there would be some corners with no value. We cannot say that the Transcendent sees more of Christ than the Traditionalist, or the Authoritarian more than the Activist. They all do their work conscious of his presence and his lordship.

But there comes a point at which the four-corner model is itself transcended. I believe that this happens when persons come to such a deep understanding of all four areas of Christian discipline that the four areas become integrated within their personalities and they find themselves at home in any position. At this point they rise to a level above the four positions, which can only be described as "being in Christ." If we were to diagram it, it might look like this:

As we seek to be "in Christ," we find ourselves raised to a level above the divisiveness of the various positions, and we discover a new unity that only the Spirit can give. I think it is no accident that the disciples had their most intimate communion with Jesus in an "upper" room. When we rise into that mystical realm where the things of earth finally achieve their proper perspective and the small priorities of our earlier life are lost in the single priority of fellowship with Christ, our grasp of the kingdom becomes too full and exciting to be confined to one position. We finally know why there are four positions, and we rejoice in the fact that God has created a variety of ways in which people can serve. We find that when we meet persons who need the touch of love, we can sit down with them in whatever position they happen to occupy at the moment and talk quietly, sharing the compassion and understanding of one who has been there. Out of a larger experience, we can focus on whatever need presents itself. Christ is free to work through us wherever we are, whatever the need may be, in whatever theological language the other person may be speaking. While we were formerly occupying one position, we seemed to be closed off from those in the rest of the church. But when we descend from the upper room of fellowship with Christ, from the table that has no separate corners, we no longer hear people speaking in the sectarian language of individual positions, but in the universal language of the need for love. And because we are in Christ, because we once held their position, we can hear them and we can be a channel through which Christ is able to bring healing. None of this comes from a sense of superiority. Rather, we recognize that while we held a particular position we felt the superiority that issued from a sense of personal, spiritual adequacy. Now, in Christ, we are aware only of our need for his adequacy, of our inability to help without first being filled with his presence. It is that need, ultimately, that defines our unity in the Spirit.

We can end our discussion in no better way than to read again the summary which Jesus gives us in Mark 12:29-31:

The most important commandment is this:
"Listen, Israel! The Lord our God is the only Lord.
    Love the Lord your God
                with all your heart,
                with all your soul,
                with all your mind,
            and with all your strength."
The second most important commandment is this:
    "Love your neighbor as you love yourself."
There is no other commandment more important than these two.

Appendix A

Finding Your Own Position

Up to this point, we have been talking theory. If we are to gain any tangible benefit from what we have been discussing, we must have a way to make some practical application of our theory. This chapter provides a way in which this can be done.

Included in the following material are an instrument for testing the position of an individual, instructions for administering and scoring the test, and a method of plotting the results in graph form. In addition, an illustrative case is presented along with suggestions for interpreting the results.

How to Decide "Which Is My Position?"

The following pages contain a test that individuals can use to determine which of the four positions they happen to be occupying at the moment.

Questionnaire

The purpose of this questionnaire is to determine your personal preferences and the needs of the congregation. **There are no right or wrong answers.** Although several answers may appeal to you, please try to choose the response that **most closely** matches your beliefs.

Circle a, b, c, or d under each question.

1. Which of the following is the most important thing our religion teaches us?

   a. The commands of God.
   b. Our duty to help others.
   c. The importance of the church.
   d. The Holy Spirit's power to change us.

2. In which of the following ways would you prefer to have your church contributions used?

   a. To set up a center to help needy people.
   b. To help build a church for my congregation.
   c. To sponsor a seminar on spiritual healing.
   d. To buy books for teaching people about God.

3. On which of the following topics would you prefer to hear your pastor preach?

   a. The things that make our denomination unique.
   b. The gifts of the Spirit.
   c. Our need to know and obey Scripture.
   d. How to help with the world's needs.

4. Which of the following is the best description of the work of Christ?

   a. He sent us the Holy Spirit to empower us.
   b. He died on the cross to save us.
   c. He taught us to care for one another.
   d. He came to show us the way to God.

5. Which of the following best describes your view of Scripture?

   a. All parts are inspired by God and are equally valuable.
   b. Some parts are no longer as relevant as they used to be; Scripture needs to be interpreted in light of the needs of today.
   c. It tells us that we are primarily spiritual beings who should spend our time in fellowship with God.
   d. It is the textbook of the faith, telling how the church came into being.

6. Which of the following do you most want the church to do for you?

   a. Inspire me to work with others to improve the world in God's name.
   b. Surround me with those who are seeking fellowship with God.
   c. Provide a place of worship and study so that I can learn what it means to be a Christian.
   d. Inform me of God's will so that I can be certain to please God.

7. Which of the following should Christian education have as its main goal?

   a. To help people study the teachings of Christ.

   b. To show people the power of God's Spirit to change them.

   c. To prepare people to help others out of love for Christ.

   d. To instruct members in the particular beliefs and interpretations of our church.

8. Which of the following is the main thing the church should do about discrimination, racism, and other examples of social injustice?

   a. Develop a network of praying people to ask God to correct the wrong.

   b. Encourage its people to take direct action to overcome the injustice, by whatever means.

   c. Sponsor programs to acquaint people with the facts.

   d. Let the legislatures and courts deal with the problem.

9. Which of the following should the church stress most heavily in its teaching?

   a. Our responsibility for others.

   b. Our duty to God.

   c. The power of the Holy Spirit to change us.

   d. The importance of the church in a Christian's life.

10. Which of these topics would you be most likely to look for in a religious education book?

   a. An interpretation of the Ten Commandments for today.

   b. Various people's experiences with Christ.

   c. Important events from church history.

   d. Jesus' teachings on social justice.

11. Which of the following would you feel most comfortable doing?

   a. Serving as a board member and helping to run the church.

   b. Being on the visitation committee for the sick and shut-in members of the church.

   c. Participating in a year-long Bible study.

   d. Being part of a regular intercessory prayer group.

12. The main purpose of the ruling board of the local church should
be to:

    a. Help members deepen their personal commitment to Christ.

    b. Make rules concerning proper belief for members.

    c. Make certain that members are shown ways to put their faith
into practice.

    d. Raise and spend money for the church; maintain the building.

13. Which person of the Trinity is most important to you?

    a. Father.

    b. Son.

    c. Holy Spirit.

14. Which of the following is the most important reason for studying
church history?

    a. To learn about my spiritual roots and to remember those who
gave me what I have.

    b. To point out where the church has failed to put Christ's teachings
to work in the world.

    c. To show us that God's power will use our work to bring about
the kingdom.

    d. To tell us what the church has discovered to be God's truth
through many ages.

15. I would rather:

    a. Listen to preaching with a congregation.

    b. Listen to an expert teach a study group.

    c. Help a needy individual, one on one.

    d. Meditate and pray by myself.

16. What is your attitude toward the idea of being ''born again''?

    a. It is meaningless unless behavior toward others also changes.

    b. It is required for salvation.

    c. It is the first step toward the baptism of the Holy Spirit.

    d. It is an emphasis made primarily by conservatives.

17. Which of the following would you rather study?

    a. Spiritual healing.

   b. Church history.

   c. Church missions.

   d. The Ten Commandments.

18. Which of the following describes most closely your idea of what it means to be a Christian?

   a. Learning and obeying the teachings of Christ as recorded in Scripture.

   b. Being part of the church, the body of Christ.

   c. Seeking fellowship with Christ in prayer and meditation.

   d. Following Christ's command to serve others in the world.

19. What is your reaction to the church actively engaging in social ministry?

   a. It is one of the main things the church should be doing.

   b. The church should stick to the gospel.

   c. Our duty is to pray for those who need help so that God will send a solution for their needs.

   d. The church should encourage individuals to be active or not, as their conscience directs them.

20. What is the most important thing the church provides for you personally?

   a. The fellowship of morning worship.

   b. The opportunity to discuss spiritual growth with others.

   c. The chance to learn how to please God.

   d. Mission outreach, at home and abroad.

21. Which statement fits you most closely?

   a. I believe that we are made in God's image and that we are to seek fellowship with God in prayer and service.

   b. I believe that the Bible contains the Word of God and that to be good Christians we are to learn God's Word and obey carefully.

   c. I believe that Jesus told us to care for others in his name and that love for others is the most important part of the gospel.

   d. I believe that the church maintains the faith from one generation to the next and that it is our duty to keep the church strong.

Administering the Test

The test answers can be marked on the test sheet itself or on an answer sheet similar to the one below.

ANSWER SHEET

Please circle only one letter for each question.

1.	a b c d	12.	a b c d
2.	a b c d	13.	a b c
3.	a b c d	14.	a b c d
4.	a b c d	15.	a b c d
5.	a b c d	16.	a b c d
6.	a b c d	17.	a b c d
7.	a b c d	18.	a b c d
8.	a b c d	19.	a b c d
9.	a b c d	20.	a b c d
10.	a b c d	21.	a b c d
11.	a b c d		

Scoring the test

Once the twenty-one responses have been obtained, they need to be entered in the scoring key. This is done by circling the appropriate letter for each question. For instance, if the response for question 1 is "a," then the letter "a" is circled for question 1 on the key.

KEY to Scoring Questionnaire

Question Number	Traditional	Authoritarian	Activist	Transcendent
1.	c	a	b	d
2.	b	d	a	c
3.	a	c	d	b
4.	d	b	c	a
5.	d	a	b	c
6.	c	d	a	b
7.	d	a	c	b
8.	c	d	b	a
9.	d	b	a	c
10.	c	a	d	b
11.	a	c	b	d
12.	d	b	c	a
13.	a	b	—	c
14.	a	d	b	c
15.	a	b	c	d
16.	d	b	a	c
17.	b	d	c	a
18.	b	a	d	c
19.	d	b	a	c
20.	a	c	d	b
TOTALS				
21.	d	b	c	a

Plotting the Spiritual Position

Total the number of circled letters in each column. The totals now need to be transferred to a grid so that the preferred position can be seen in graph form. The plotting grid looks like this.

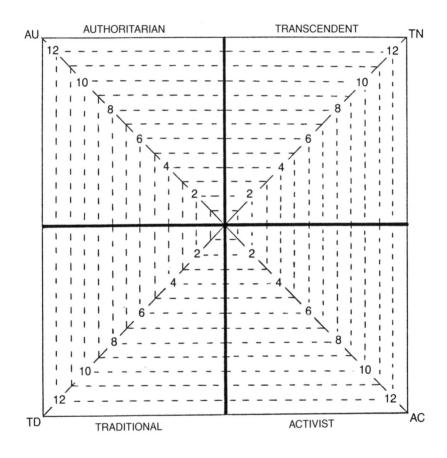

Sample Test Results

1. Let us use as an example the following answer sheet.

1. b	6. d	11. a	16. a
2. c	7. a	12. c	17. a
3. d	8. c	13. a	18. b
4. c	9. a	14. d	19. b
5. b	10. c	15. b	20. b
			21. c

2. The results would be entered in the key as follows:

Question Number	Traditional	Authoritarian	Activist	Transcendent
1.	c	a	(b)	d
2.	b	d	a	(c)
3.	a	c	(d)	b
4.	d	b	(c)	a
5.	d	a	(b)	c
6.	c	(d)	a	b
7.	d	(a)	c	b
8.	(c)	d	b	a
9.	d	b	(a)	c
10.	(c)	a	d	b
11.	(a)	c	b	d
12.	d	b	(c)	a
13.	(a)	b	—	c
14.	a	(d)	b	c
15.	a	(b)	c	d
16.	d	b	(a)	c
17.	b	d	c	(a)
18.	(b)	a	d	c
19.	d	(b)	a	c
20.	a	c	d	(b)
TOTALS	*5*	*5*	*7*	*3*
21.	d	b	(c)	a

3. The totals for questions 1 through 20 would then be plotted on the grid. Each of the four numbers is used to complete a square in the appropriate corner of the grid. The "5" under "Traditional" would be entered on the grid by completing the #5 square on the grid (between "4" and "6") in the Traditional corner; the "5" under "Authoritarian" would be a similar size square in the Authoritarian corner; and so on. You will see that the results graphically show the preferences for the Activist position.

Finally, question 21 is used as a check on the responses to questions 1 through 20. If it matches the dominant position, it adds strength to the subject's position; if it differs, it indicates a broader mixture of beliefs. Since the response to question 21 is in the Activist column, the "AC" at the corner of the Activist position is circled. The dominant square has been marked with its initials, in this case "AC," in order to identify the various positions in a large sample more quickly. The completed grid will look like this.

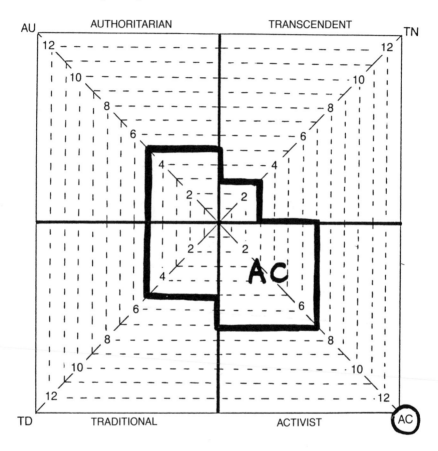

Interpreting the Test Results

Examination of the completed grid reveals several things:

a. While the AC is dominant, both the TD and AU are a strong second, showing a mix of values.

b. The weakest of the four areas is the TN, which may inspire the individual to think about the need to grow in that direction.

c. The agreement of question 21 with the test results strengthens the AC profile of the subject. If 21 were not AC, it could (1) indicate that the person simply preferred another definition, (2) indicate that while testing AC, the person does not feel comfortable with that definition, or (3) reflect a strong secondary point of view. None of these results are "right" or "wrong"; they merely add greater dimension to the individual profile.

We might think that an ideal response would be an equal total for each area, showing perfect balance in all four quadrants. This would be plotted by a square entirely around the grid at number 5. However, it is not expected that anyone will indicate that he or she is perfectly balanced in all areas. The purpose of the test is to discover the dominant position and to indicate areas for growth.

Appendix B

Putting the Theory to Work

An old church, in the center of town, calls a new pastor, a liberal who sees an opportunity to minister to the decaying inner city. The traditional members, many of whom have fled to the suburbs, want to continue sponsoring programs exclusively for the members of the congregation. After some initial conflict, the minister convinces a majority of the members that the church has a responsibility to the community in which it exists. They open the building to neighborhood children and other needy groups and find a new sense of enthusiasm and vitality in the congregation.

○The ruling board of a local congregation, charged with the spiritual oversight of the church, administers educational programs and fosters spiritual growth among the members, while the board of trustees attends to the financial and property matters. A proposal to combine the boards to foster administrative efficiency results in the board spending most of its time dealing with financial matters to the exclusion of spiritual concerns. As a consequence, some of the members resign, concerned that the church has forgotten its spiritual priorities.

○A church's new worship chairperson, a woman, has a strongly nonsexist position and proposes that the service be redesigned. She modifies the liturgy, rewords the old hymns, and insists on inclusive language in the Scripture lesson. The proposed changes catch the minister's imagination and are put into practice. However, the members of the congregation are disturbed by the innovations and voice their protests loudly.

○A minister who has served a local church for a number of years develops a charismatic point of view and begins preaching heavily on the subject. He gathers around him a group of people who believe as he does and spends a large part of his time training them to be more vocal in their beliefs. The group begins to teach that everyone in the congregation should adopt its point of view. The result is a split in the congregation and a mass exodus of members.

○A church custodian continually makes requests to the minister for permission to get equipment, to change procedures, and to relay information to the congregation. The minister continually tells him that such authority resides in the ruling board and that the custodian will have to go through channels. Since the board meets at night and the custodian works only daylight hours, there is a constant tension between the two staff members, the custodian complaining that the minister is a poor leader and indifferent to the needs of the staff.

○A minister, who has spent a large part of her time enabling spiritual growth groups in which people set their own goals, is succeeded by a new pastor whose strength is in preaching and teaching. In addition, the new pastor is accustomed to doing the administrative work of the congregation by himself. He begins his new ministry by issuing directives for the committees to follow, disbanding the study groups, and laying heavy emphasis in his sermons on what his hearers must believe and do in order to be acceptable to God. The uproar that ensues results in a number of the people leaving. Other people are attracted, however, because of the stronger evangelistic program, and the church takes on a new life.

●   ●   ●   ●   ●

Do some of these situations sound familiar to you? Each of these scenarios demonstrates the dynamics of our four positions at work. Some of them show what happens when the positions are ignored, and some suggest how the different positions can be used to broaden the church's ministry.

How can we make practical use of the four-position model we have been considering? There are at least four ways in which this approach can be used in a local church: by the pastor, by the ruling board, by the congregation as a whole, and by individual members in study groups.

The Pastor

The pastor is in a position to apply the insights of the four-position model in a number of ways.

A. The first step would involve the pastor's taking the test to determine his or her own dominant position. If the pastor finds a high degree of balance in his or her theological position, that fact will suggest one course of action. If he or she is settled firmly in one position, another course of action will be needed.

1. If the pastor is fairly well balanced between the four positions, he or she may want to introduce a program that will help the congregation learn the interrelationship of all four positions so the members will come to value the differing gifts of various people.

2. If the pastor is heavily invested in only one of the areas, he or she may want to bring greater balance to the church's program by arranging to have on the ruling board those whose dominant position is different from his or her own.

B. In either case, it would be helpful if the ruling board and then the entire congregation could be tested. This would provide the pastor with essential information for planning the next steps.

1. Testing the board would produce the following information: it would reveal whether one of the positions dominates the board; it would show whether the majority of members are in a position similar to or different from the pastor's; it would indicate whether one of the positions has been neglected in the program planning of the board; and it would help the pastor to know whether the board members had been put on committees appropriate to their preferred position.

2. Test results from the congregation as a whole will tell the pastor what the majority expects from his or her preaching, whether unrecognized position imbalances are responsible for certain long-standing congregational problems, and which areas are underrepresented in the congregational profile. This last information will suggest specific directions in which the pastor may want to help the people of the congregation move toward a fuller ministry.

C. With this information in hand, the pastor can then ask the essential question, Where am I in relation to the members of the board and the congregation? While it might seem ideal for the pastor to be perfectly balanced in all four positions, the reality is that most of us lean moderately or heavily toward a particular position. Since this is the result of a variety of influences over a number of years, it is not likely that we will change quickly simply by having our position brought to our attention. Rather, we need to accept our position as well as that of others. We want to learn to work with them, not in spite of the differences but because we see those differences providing a balancing factor for our own imbalance. Thus, it is not essential that the pastor be in the same position as the congregation or the board, but simply that he or she be aware of their relative positions.

D. The pastor who has been troubled by conflicts between herself or himself and certain individuals or groups within the congregation might want to analyze those conflicts by using the theory in this book. Issues that may have been written off as personality clashes may have deeper philosophical causes. Understanding why others respond in fundamentally different ways to certain issues may provide the pastor with a new tool for encouraging peace and cooperation.

One pastor who was a Republican felt the need to preach from time to time on social issues, emphasizing the need to use the country's limited resources for human betterment rather than adding to an already overgrown military establishment. One of his faithful elders believed in the priority of a strong military, complete with the latest in weapons technology. He wrote the pastor after one sermon, accusing him of being a Democrat because of his liberal views and pleading for balance in his preaching. The pastor sat down with the man, diagramed the four positions, and indicated that the elder's legitimate concern for national security belonged in the Authoritarian position. He then described the Activist position, repeating Jesus' statement that we are caring for him when we care for others. The pastor explained that the sermon had come from the Activist point of view. He went on to point out that certain previous sermons had emphasized other positions, revealing to the elder his effort to minister to all points of view in the congregation. The conversation helped eliminate the misunderstanding between them. However, as they parted, the elder commented that it had been a long time since he had heard an Authoritarian sermon, pointing out that the pastor was a Transcendent who avoided an Authoritarian stance. Thus, both men learned something valuable from the encounter.

E. This kind of insight is another benefit the pastor can gain from having the questionnaire information at hand. If the pastor is strongly convinced that one position is more important than the rest, does he or she preach sermons in that area exclusively, disregarding the needs of those in the congregation who have other positions?

One example of this is the case of a charismatic pastor who spends most of his time preaching about the gifts of the Spirit and neglecting the more practical concerns of the kingdom and the church. If he is strongly Transcendent, he may be seen as impractical and irrelevant by those in the other three corners. If he has a strong Authoritarian element added to his Pentecostalism, he will immediately disenchant those with other positions by demanding that they see things from his point of view. The Authoritarians in the congregation, particularly, may claim that he is unscriptural in his emphasis, and the ensuing divisions can be fatal to a congregation.

A pastor needs to be aware of hidden bias, based on a preference he or she may never have confronted. A minister is called to be pastor to all the people and needs to feed the whole flock, not just the sheep who congregate in one particular corner of the pen.

1. An Authoritarian may tend to be heavy on righteousness and punishment while there are those in the congregation starving for forgiveness.

2. A Traditionalist may expound at length about theology and the need for money, anxious to keep the institution on an even keel, while in the pews there are those whose excitement about their personal faith is gradually cooling because of his unimaginative and impersonal approach.

3. An Activist, feeling that nothing is more important than a practical application of Jesus' teachings in a needy world, may preach heavily on social justice and political action, feeding people strong meat before they learn to digest the basic milk of the gospel, which will help them grow into mature—and, therefore, more active—Christians.

4. A Transcendent, ecstatic in a personal relationship with God in Christ, may think only of his or her own experience and ignore the differing states of spiritual growth among the members. By assuming too much, this pastor can actually turn off some of the people, frightening them by an overabundance of zeal rather than bringing them closer to Christ.

F. Realizing this need for balance, and the possibility of neglecting certain areas, the pastor can then ask herself (or himself) which positions need to be strengthened in the pulpit and in program planning and which groups she (or he) may have been consciously or unconsciously ignoring in pastoral work.

If there is a small charismatic group in the congregation that has been meeting privately, has the pastor attended its meetings or talked to some of the members, particularly if he is an Authoritarian or a Traditionalist? If not, is it because he disagrees with them? Perhaps intimate discussions might help inform him of their sincerity or give him an opportunity to strengthen their orthodoxy. Has it been because he is afraid that they might expect certain things from him that he does not want to give? They are still part of his flock and have a right to expect loving concern, regardless of his position—and theirs.

If the pastor is an Activist, is she aware of a group of Authoritarians in the congregation who are disaffected by her liberalism and social emphasis? Has she sought out these people, not just to justify her position, but to hear them express what they need from her? She has a duty to preach and live as God directs her, and no group in the congregation should attempt to make her act against her conscience. But if fear of disagreement or avoidance of honest struggle keeps her from sharing herself with them, she is neglecting her responsibility. While she must speak the words of God as she hears them, she must also minister to those who hear God speaking different words. The most effective pastor is the one who can reach out to all people while at the same time retaining his or her unique view of the gospel of Jesus Christ. This is not an impossible task; it requires most of all the gift of patient listening.

The Ruling Board

One of the most important places to study the interaction of the four positions is on the ruling board (the session, consistory, diaconate, administrative commission—whatever you may call it in your denomination). Diversity within the congregation may not have an immediate effect on the running of the church. Most congregations, however, are governed by a handful of elected individuals, men and women each characterized by a unique combination of attitudes, and their responses to the pastor's initiatives in leading the church will be shaped by the position they hold.

A. First, of course, the pastor will want to test the entire board to discover its composite profile. If new members are elected to the board each year, it would be wise to re-administer the test annually to all the members, including those who have taken it before. Response to the test is a subtle thing that may vary from time to time, and it is helpful to give individuals an opportunity to reexamine their responses. Re-administering the test also measures long-term changes in a person's position.

B. After the test has been administered, the pastor will want to take time to explain the theory to the board members, pointing out the four areas that should be covered in the church's work and that, in some combinations, should be present in every member's personal religious makeup. The pastor may want to underline the consequences that occur when a church ignores one of these areas in its ministry.

C. When the results are tabulated, it is helpful to diagram them on a grid similar to the one used to illustrate an individual's position. If there are fifteen members on the board—for instance, 6 Traditionalists, 4 Authoritarians, 2 Activists, and 3 Transcendents—those numbers could be transposed onto the grid to illustrate the "personality" of the board as a whole (see diagram 1a). This profile could then be displayed alongside the pastor's profile (diagram 1b) and the two diagrams compared. In the case of these examples, it is obvious that the board is weakest at the very point where the pastor is strongest. Depending on the approach of the pastor and the attitude of the board, this can be an advantage or potential trouble.

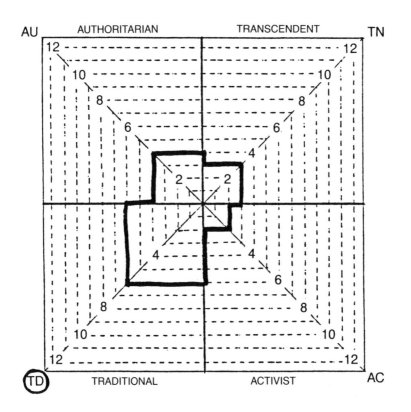

1a. Ruling Board

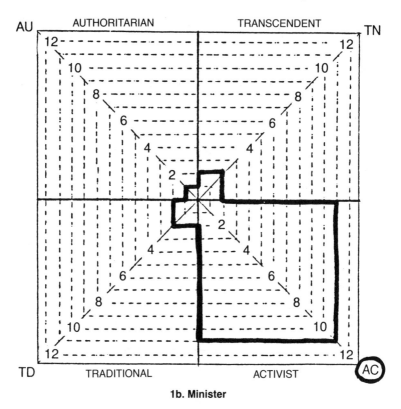

1b. Minister

1. If the pastor is a dominant person who expects to make the decisions and have the board follow along, most of the members are going to be working against their consciences, or at the least agreeing without much enthusiasm. As a result, the pastor may find much of his work to be an uphill pull against widespread indifference or concerted opposition.

2. The pastor may be content to let the board do the work of administration while she acts as a resource. This particular combination can add balance to the board as a whole. Each can remind the other of areas of concern that they might ignore if left to themselves.

D. The next step would be to consider which areas have been slighted and which have had the strongest emphasis. If the majority on the board are Traditionalists while the pastor is a Transcendent and if there are no Activists on the board, this fact will come to light immediately. An examination of the programming decisions of the previous year will help highlight the consequences of this type of board composition. Has the board spent a large proportion of its time dealing with financial matters? Is the pastor primarily interested in leading groups, in meeting with people for spiritual direction, and in planning worship experiences and retreats? In other words, do most of the board's decisions deal with those who are already members of the church to the exclusion of those outside the church? Scriptural passages could be considered in subsequent meetings to remind the members of their duty to the lost, the needy, the friend-less. How could the church change its focus from its own people and property to those who have no one to care for them? In what concrete ways could the church broaden its ministry to reach out to these people?

E. A further step is an examination of the correspondence between the individual position-preference of a board member and his or her committee assignment. Most of the administrative and program tasks supervised by the board fall naturally into one of the four positions.

1. Financial matters, care of the building, establishment of rules for use of the facilities, all fall naturally into the Traditional position.

2. The broad range of Christian education fits into the Authoritarian position and is best accomplished by those who have a clear sense of theological truth and a desire to see that truth shared with others.

3. Mission work, both at home and abroad, is a concern of the Activist position when it is seen, not as a means of forcing one's theological position on others, but as a means of caring for people in need.

4. Evangelism is a function of the Transcendent position when it is concerned with helping an individual make a commit-ment rather than convincing him or her to adopt a particular theology. Spiritual growth also falls into this area.

Especially in 3 and 4 above, we need to note carefully the hidden influence of the Authoritarian attitude. If it is present as a strong secondary factor in another position, it may cause an Activist or a Transcendent to say, "This is the only way!" instead of, "This is one way." This temptation can convert concern for others into self-righteousness so that the subtle differences in the other positions are obscured by the effort to demonstrate that "my position's better than yours!''

In addition to the areas listed above, other areas such as worship are strongly influenced by the preference of those providing the leadership. Worship designed by those with a Traditional leaning will be denominational and will tend to resist change. However, if someone in the Transcendent position, for instance, is responsible for what happens in worship, the service will probably have a more personal flavor with an emphasis on individual response. An Activist as chairperson of the Finance Committee may urge greater benevolence giving, while the Traditionalists on that committee will react by demanding that excess funds be invested to produce long-term income.

The pastor may decide to use in the various committee positions people with a strong preference in that area in order to get more directive leadership, or the pastor may put a person on a committee that challenges her past thinking, stimulating her to grow at the same time she brings a new approach to that committee's work.

F. An examination of the board's composition may suggest changes that need to be made.

1. If it is decided that certain areas have been slighted in the past, the board may want to add new members from segments of the congregation not previously represented on the board.

2. A study of the four-position structure might cause individuals to recognize underdeveloped areas in their own spiritual makeup which need work.

3. A broader awareness can be cultivated by a time of study at the beginning of the board's meetings, in which those from different positions have the opportunity to talk to one another, individually or in small groups. In this way members can learn more about the thinking of those in other positions.

4. Outside speakers can be brought in for motivational and informational presentations during an enrichment period at the beginning of the meeting, representing various positions, especially those that have been neglected or misunderstood in the past. A missionary, an investment counselor, a visiting nurse, a person who does spiritual healing, a juvenile officer—all could broaden the viewpoint of the members and suggest directions in which the board could move with a new sense of creativity. A diagram of the four positions could be posted in the board room to remind the group of its overall responsibility and to help members decide

where the current work fits into the fuller ministry of the church.

G. The board may decide to test the entire congregation in order to learn more about the viewpoints of its members. That possibility will be considered here rather than under a separate heading because the board itself will most likely make use of the material thus generated.

1. If a graph similar to the one made for the ruling board (diagram 1a) is made for the congregation, it can easily be determined whether the board's representation matches the congregation's composition as a whole. In this case it may be preferable to have dissimilarity on the board. If the congregation does not elect to its board people who feel more strongly than the average members or those who are better balanced in their position preferences, the congregation may tend to stagnate and settle into a comfortable routine that challenges no one.

2. The board needs to determine whether the congregation is lopsided in its overall makeup. Is it Traditional to the exclusion of the Transcendent? Is it so Authoritarian that it neglects its Activist duty? The board has an obligation to provide gentle leadership in areas that may have been slighted.

3. How does the congregation's dominant position affect the preaching program, the focus of Christian education, the activities of the church's groups? Do those emphases need to be changed? Do they confirm people in their present positions or encourage movement and growth?

4. What rifts exist in the congregation? Can they be explained by clashes of position preferences? Seeing the conflicts in these terms may suggest new ways to deal with them, one of which is described in the following section on small groups.

5. This information contains great educational value for the congregation. It is a simple way to share with the members the breadth of a full ministry, the role each individual plays in that ministry, and the contributions which are made by those in other positions.

6. Sharing with the congregation the diagram of the four positions will help explain why certain changes in emphasis are being made by the board so as to insure that all the elements of heart-soul-mind-strength are covered by what the church does for its people and its community.

SMALL GROUPS
Using the Test

Many churches have discovered the value of small groups for
fostering individual spiritual growth. Our model adapts itself well
to the small-group process and, because of the intimacy of the group
approach, can produce lasting insights.

It is assumed that those in the small group have come together
because of their desire to learn and their willingness to grow. Therefore, the approach can be somewhat more intense than in other
learning situations.

The following suggestions are directed to the person(s) responsible
for leading the group.

1. The first step would be to administer the test to all the members
of the group.

2. After the test has been completed, someone who clearly un-
derstands the model should give a careful presentation of the structure, showing how the varying points of view fit into the larger
whole. It is suggested that this interpretive material be presented
following the administration of the test, in order to prevent individuals from skewing the results by trying to guess which answer fits
a certain category.

3. Groups may be formed at this time. If there are only a few
people, you may want to keep everyone together. If there are eight
or more participants, you might consider small groups of four or
five people each. Consider dividing the people according to their
test results so that a variety of positions are represented in each
group. This makes for more stimulating conversation.

4. Begin the group sharing by having the members react to the
results of the test. Do they agree that they belong in the positions
in which the test places them? If the members know one another,
have them give their opinions as to whether the position fits the
individual or not, giving reasons why: "Yes, I think you are a
Traditionalist; you've been a trustee for years." "No, I think you're
more of an Activist than a Transcendent; you spend so much time
helping outside the church." Make certain that the members have
a sheet of paper that explains and contrasts the four positions, so
that they can refer to the differences during their discussion.

5. Let the members each give a short history of their faith development and participation in the church. Then have them answer
this question: How does all this explain the position in which I find

myself today?

6. If they haven't already done so, ask them to think of the influence of parents and other significant authority figures in their developing years, relating that history to their current position. Then pose this question: As you understand the positions, in which position would you put your mother and father, your childhood pastor, and other influential adults?

7. Have them ask themselves if they have always held their current position, or whether at different times in their lives they occupied others. Ask: Which other positions have you been in? What caused you to change? How do you feel about those who are now in that former position? Do you understand them or look down on them? Why?

8. Now have them spend some time talking about their different ways of seeing things. This needs to be done carefully, with an emphasis on the fact that there is no one right way to think but that all points of view have validity. No one should attempt to convert the others. Each should express his or her point of view as clearly as possible so that he or she, as well as the group, will understand why he or she holds that position. Have group members review some of the test questions to which they gave differing answers, explaining why they answered as they did.

Striving for Growth

If the group wishes to go deeper, the members can look for spiritual imbalances in their particular position, sharing with one another the reasons for choosing or resisting other positions.

1. Have them ask: What sort of gaps do I detect in my own theological position? If I have been involved personally in two of the positions, what do I think of the other two? (I didn't realize they existed, I think they are worthless, I'm afraid of investigating them, etc.)

2. If anyone expresses fear or doubt about a certain position, have the person develop that feeling. Then allow someone who holds that position to share feelings about that area of faith for the purpose of reducing the tensions and misunderstanding of the first person.

3. Each person might conclude by suggesting ways in which he or she could broaden his or her point of view, specifically by incorporating into his or her outlook the viewpoint of a certain position he or she now ignores. How might one do this? How could the church help one in this effort? How have the person's attitudes

changed concerning those in the church who think differently?
The Use of Stories

Since narrative is an effective means of sharing truth, the group
at this point might attempt to increase its understanding of the varying
points of view through the use of stories.

1. Have each member think of a story that best illustrates his or
her involvement in his or her particular position.

a. A Traditionalist might tell about her memories of church
groups as a youth, a particularly memorable worship service, a
trip to see a meaningful historic place.

b. An Authoritarian might remember a Bible study in college
that caught his excitement, a class he once taught, a moment
when the truth became particularly clear for him.

c. An Activist will perhaps think of a group with which she
worked in the community, a family helped in a dramatic way and
the effect of their reaction on her, or her desire to help change
the world in certain respects.

d. A Transcendent may speak of the memory of spiritual
breakthroughs, a conversation with a friend that opened a door,
the first time he caught a sense of the unity of all people under a
loving God.

It is important that the categories not be defined too tightly. It is
probable that a particular story will have elements of several positions
in it. This indicates the ultimate unity of the entire design and the
relative falseness of attempting to separate them too completely. The
same story might make two individuals think of two different positions. What is important is the interpretation that each person gives
to the story he or she relates.

2. Now have the members consider four parables, asking whether
they illustrate the various positions.

a. Traditional: The elder brother in the story of the prodigal
son (Luke 15:11-32). While it is customary to be critical of the
elder brother, there are some positive things to be said for his
point of view. Does the Traditionalist in the group tend to see
himself in somewhat the same position, trying to tend the shop
while other people run off into exotic experiences and then come
home sadder but wiser? Does she feel unappreciated while others
flaunt a more dramatic faith style? Does she see her work as
satisfying and important while others have escaped to a far country
and look down on her style of faith?

    b. Authoritarian: The parable of the sower and the four soils (Mark 4:1-9, 13-20). Read this parable in terms of its "dos and don'ts." Jesus is clearly saying that certain lifestyles are wrong and others are preferable. Does the Authoritarian in the group feel that certain emphases in the church are "rocky ground" or "thorn bushes" that choke out the truth? What is his definition of good soil? What does he think Jesus was trying to say about the right way of living the truth?

    c. Activist: The story of the good Samaritan (Luke 10:25-37). Ask the Activist in the group about her reaction to this story and whether it expresses her feeling about what Jesus wants us to do. Who are the victims in today's world? Whom would Jesus want the good Samaritan to help in modern America? What about the liberalism in Jesus' praise of one who was considered unclean by traditional Jews? Who might Jesus praise today, shocking the conservatives in the church? Does the Activist feel that the priests and the Levites still walk by on the other side of the road? In what way?

    d. Transcendent: The parable of the hidden treasure (Matthew 13:44-45). Does the group's Transcendent think he has found a secret treasure of which many in the church are still unaware? What is it? Has he hidden it, or does he share it with everyone? What happens when he shares it? Do people accept it eagerly or reject it? Does he understand the idea of selling everything in order to possess this treasure? How has he done this? How did he find the treasure in the first place?

Conclusion

If we take seriously Paul's statement that we are one in the Spirit, then we need to come to a broader understanding of the differences that frequently divide us. Our ignorance and our selfishness too often keep us isolated from one another and contradict our assertion that Christ died for all of us.

Our basic sin is to think that our little sliver of truth is the whole truth. We will have taken a mighty leap forward when we realize that we are all part of a truth far greater than any of us can fully comprehend. Acknowledging that the truth we understand fits into an important place in the comprehensive truth of God can at once teach us humility and elevate our significance.

In the same way that we cannot conduct four full-time careers simultaneously, no one of us can invest herself or himself with equal vigor in all aspects of God's work at the same moment. At one point in our life, we will be more interested in one phase of the work; at another point, some other form of spiritual expression will catch our imagination. It may be that striving for perfect balance will create in us a kind of paralysis; imbalance obviously creates energy and change much as the law of entropy powers the universe by its disequilibrium: when the universe reaches balance, the available energy will disappear and the world will cease. Each of us needs to be a charged particle, energized by our present position, so that the overall balance in the church can be made up of dynamic parts. If we were in perfect equilibrium as individuals, the church might be robbed of its essential energy.

The most we can hope for is that at some time during our lives, we will have held each of the four positions. This process can show us where we are most comfortable and at the same time can teach us to appreciate the gifts of those in the other three positions. In any event, most of us are a unique combination of dominant and secondary attitudes. Accepting that uniqueness, seeing it as our bequest to the world, can be the greatest thing we do for God and for God's people.

Thus, I may never see my true completeness in a single moment. I may only glimpse it as I look back on a lifetime of struggle and service during which the various positions have succeeded one another in my experience.

In any present moment, however, a large degree of balance is provided by my spiritual community. I give that community whatever is the dominant position in my life at the moment, while other people add the other three. When I know this, I begin to comprehend Paul's phrase "the body of Christ." I do not despise the other positions; I need their perspectives as much as they need mine. The fact that they do their work frees me to exercise more fully the ministry of my own position. I need to thank God constantly for that richness rather than criticize others for not thinking as I do. If the whole church sat in my pew, it would collapse!

On an even larger scale, the various denominations divide among them the four essential areas of ministry. Mainline churches tend to cluster in the Traditional area; apostolic and fundamentalist churches provide the Authoritarian influence (which explains why liberation theology and other modern influences are causing such a stir); liberal churches are traditionally more Activist than others, both in their theology and their social consciousness; and Pentecostal churches are more squarely in the Transcendent position than many others. Of course, all denominations include all four influences, but each seems to have its area of special emphasis. Thus, the whole church of Christ worldwide creates its own corporate balance. When we reject any part of it in superiority or narrow-mindedness, we reject part of the body to which we ourselves belong.

The work of the Spirit is seen in the slow process by which all of these influences are spreading through all churches without regard to tradition, creating a kind of universal recognition of the value of all the positions. We still have a long way to go, but it should be our prayer that the day will come when we will no longer say, ''My way is better than yours,'' but rather ask, ''Lord, make us one,'' because we have learned to embrace those in all four positions with equal respect and love.

When that happens, the kingdom will have come because we will finally recognize that we are all one.

73632

Notes

Chapter 2

[1] John B. Cobb, Jr., *Varieties of Protestantism* (Philadelphia: The Westminster Press, 1960), p. 94.

Chapter 5

[1] John Killinger, in a sermon entitled "The Packaging of the Gospel," *Pulpit Digest*, vol. 65, no. 473 (May–June 1985), p. 55. Copyright © 1985 by *Pulpit Digest*. Used by permission.

[2] Robert C. Shannon, "Let Me Illustrate," *Pulpit Digest*, vol. 59, no. 436 (March–April 1979), p. 44. Copyright © 1979 by *Pulpit Digest*. Used by permission.

Chapter 7

[1] Carl G. Jung, *Modern Man in Search of a Soul*, trans. W. S. Dell and Cary F. Baynes (New York: Harcourt Brace Jovanovich, Inc., 1933), p. 93.

[2] The type descriptions that follow are taken from two sources: David Keirsey and Marilyn Bates, *Please Understand Me: Character and Temperament Types* (Del Mar, Calif.: Prometheus Nemesis Book Co., Inc., 1984), pp. 16-22; and Gordon Lawrence, *People Types and Tiger Stripes* 2nd ed. (Gainesville, Fla.: Center for Applications of Psychological Type, Inc., 1982), pp. 7-8.

[3] Keirsey and Bates, *Please Understand Me*, p. 17.

[4] Halford E. Luccock, Exposition of "The Gospel According to St. Mark," *The Interpreter's Bible*, vol. 7 (Nashville: Abingdon-Cokesbury Press, 1951), p. 848.

262
SL63

73632

DATE DUE

NOV 25 '8?			

DEMCO 38-297